KU-845-092

PARLIAMENTARY GOVERNMENT IN FRANCE:

Revolutionary Origins, 1789-1791

BY R. K. GOOCH

Professor of Political Science in
the University of Virginia

Cornell University Press

ITHACA, NEW YORK

© 1960 by Cornell University

CORNELL UNIVERSITY PRESS

First published 1960

This work has been brought to
publication with the assistance of
a grant from the Ford Foundation.

C

204795
Modern History

PRINTED IN THE UNITED STATES OF AMERICA
BY THE VAIL-BALLOU PRESS, INC.

LC60008281

UNIVERSITY
LIBRARY
NOTTINGHAM

Preface

PERHAPS a word about the inception of this book is not inappropriate. A little over thirty-five years ago I became interested in French government and politics, and began some study of them. There resulted a series of several books and a substantially larger number of articles. Increasing emphasis was placed on the French parliamentary system, particularly on the largely indigenous regime that was developed during the Third Republic. A short time before the Second World War I had the impulse to undertake a history of parliamentary government in France. To this end I managed again to spend a year in France. The plan was to follow the conventional French practice of beginning with the Restoration, and fairly wide-ranging researches were undertaken in accordance with this pattern. The idea gradually crystallized that it would be worth while to make an earlier start and, more specifically, to write an account of the first two years of the Revolution. The simple consideration was appearance of interesting evidence that certain Revolutionary leaders possessed a striking understanding of the essentials of the system which was being evolved in England, that those essentials were in considerable measure actually put into practice in France during the years 1789–1791, and that

v

there developed even this early certain tendencies toward modification which have prevailed down to the present time.

My altered plan was being followed when the Second World War caused first its partial neglect and then its complete abandonment. After nearly ten years, I was fortunate enough to be awarded one of the first Fulbright Research Fellowships in France, with a view to making some general study of the new Fourth Republic. On this occasion, I revived as a by-product, so to say, interest in the earlier historical project. The result was a resumption in rare spare time of study and writing during a few more years. It would be a miracle if the final product failed to display a number of results of the unfortunately interrupted procedure I was constrained to follow. I can hope for no more than that much effort to reduce the defects to a minimum was partially successful.

My initial study in France and more recent brief opportunities to pursue the study were made possible by assistance from an organization at the University of Virginia and from its helpful and sympathetic long-time director, their names now being conjoined as the Wilson Gee Institute for Research in Social Science. Invaluable aid in typing and in other respects was over a long period given to me without stint by the secretary of the Institute, Miss Ruth Ritchie; and the final draft of my manuscript was most expertly typed by Mrs. Thomas E. Gay of the Office of the Dean of the College. To them both I am most grateful.

R. K. G.

University of Virginia
8 February 1960

Contents

vii

PARLIAMENTARY GOVERNMENT IN FRANCE:

Revolutionary Origins, 1789–1791

Introduction

WHEN the imperial regime in Russia was tottering on the brink of revolution, the Tsarina vigorously urged her consort to stand firm against *ministerial responsibility*, about which, she asserted, "all" had "gone mad." The symbolic significance of this stubbornly reactionary resistance to a political concept is as simple as it is far-reaching. In the context of European constitutional history, hostility to every form of political absolutism is a function of aspirations toward political democracy; and, as it happens, political democracy is in Europe identified for practical purposes with a system of government that is characterized by a specific concept of ministerial responsibility.

It would be the work of supererogation to list the European states—and, indeed, parts of states, as in Germany—in which cabinet or parliamentary government prevails. Switzerland aside, wherever conditions exist that are such as to warrant designating a European state as in a general sense free, there the parliamentary system will be found to be the accepted political regime. Moreover, wherever a state has lost its freedom, the parliamentary system will be found in some manner to have been overthrown; and, if "laws of history" exist, then the prophecy may be confidently set down that wherever a European state which is not now free may gain or regain political liberty, there the parliamentary system of government is sure to be established. Parliamentary government, a French writer once asserted, is that to which "every civilization turns or returns."[1] This is merely to repeat that in Europe political democracy has come to be identified with parliamentary government.

Parliamentary Government: English Origins

As is well known, the parliamentary regime is a product of English institutional and constitutional history. Obscure and controversial corners of the picture will doubtless continue to exist, but general agreement prevails concerning essentials. When, at the time of the Glorious Revolution, monarchy was retained in spite of recognition that ultimate power was for practical purposes to belong to Parliament, a problem of reconciliation manifestly was posed. Groping attempts to solve the problem appeared at once, but the course of the eighteenth century saw only the important beginnings of a solution the full development of which has continued to the present day.

If it is a commonplace that parliamentary government represents historically a reconciliation of the powers of king and parliament, analysis, supplementing history, may suggest various other formulations of the problem. Parliamentary government was—the tense is still historical—a solution evoked for reconciling monarchy and representative government. In turn, representative government, unless the shift from history to analysis involves too great a risk of anachronism, may be identified with aspirations toward political democracy, in which case the reconciliation is one of monarchy and political democracy. In somewhat philosophical

[1] Paul de Rémusat, *A. Thiers* (Paris, 1889), p. 136.

terms, parliamentary government is a reconciliation—or an attempted reconciliation—of the principles of unity and diversity. Plato somewhere has Socrates pay high tribute to the man who can reconcile the one and the many; and, in this context, parliamentary government appears as something to praise as well as to analyze and to understand. Finally, parliamentary government is—the emphasis now being strongly on analysis—one solution of the largely modern question of what kind of relationship should exist between the law-making and the law-enforcing authorities in the state. The solution involves a combination—one thinks of Bagehot's reference to the cabinet as a buckle that binds—of principle and practice, of theory and fact.

Parliamentary Government: French Influence

Although real measurement of influence is an exceedingly difficult thing, there can be little doubt but that European views concerning the relationship of parliamentary government and political democracy are, like ideas in many realms, derived primarily from France. In matters of government, France has herself certainly been influenced by England; but where British influence has extended to the rest of Europe, the impact has on the whole been indirectly from Britain, directly from France. A very simple but perhaps not greatly oversimplified consideration in the matter is that France has, with no little success, reduced to written form the essentials of the "unwritten" Constitution of England, and other European countries have adopted and adapted French models.

If parliamentary government deserves praise as being something more than a historical reconciliation of monarchy and democracy, if as a solution of a basic governmental problem it has merits of its own, then connection of the regime with monarchy is not a necessary relationship. This is clearly an important consideration in the history of France and of Europe. The parliamentary system of the Third Republic was, as is well known, the first example in history of the operation of parliamentary government in the absence of monarchy. The fact that a combination at that time of republicanism and parliamentarism gave to France the longest-lived governmental system in the period since the Old Regime is a simple explanation of the relative weakness of monarchical sentiment in twentieth-century France. So also, it goes far to explain the establishment of parliamentary republics in other countries of Europe, not only since the Second World War but even in the period between the Wars. All this may perhaps be formulated as another "law of history": If the identification of parliamentary government and political democracy is, for historical reasons in a given state, not attended by a further identification of republicanism and political democracy, parliamentary government may be sufficiently, though not wholly, justified as an instrument for reconciling a traditional and a modern system; whereas if conditions are such that monarchy is felt to be unacceptable, the parliamentary system must be justified in terms of its intrinsic merits.

Parliamentary Government in France: Historical Development

Among various patterns that have been suggested as aids to seeing some coherence in the apparent chaos of French constitutional history since the Revolution, by no means least interesting is a schematic plan offered by the late Professor Maurice Hauriou in terms of parliamentary government.[2] The outline is based on the proposition that parliamentary government has been introduced into France

---

[2] See his *Précis de droit constitutionnel* (2d ed.; Paris, 1929), pp. 293 ff.

on two occasions—at the time of the Restoration and at the time of the establishment of the Third Republic. Subsequent to these events, following the fall of the First and of the Second Empires, France experienced periods of relative governmental stability. In each instance, the stability was to be explained in terms of an equilibrium resulting from a reconciliation of extremes, which in combination realized a viability possible to neither of the extremes by itself. The extremes, in turn, were the omnipotence of a sovereign assembly and the dictatorship of a single executive. The first cycle of sovereign assembly, executive dictatorship, and parliamentary regime, a cycle which extended from 1789 to 1848, failed to reach complete equilibrium because parliamentary government was not founded on the democratic basis of universal suffrage.[3] Inasmuch as, in the second cycle, the parliamentary Regime under the Third Republic does not suffer from such a disability, it is in principle definitive.

A contention could hardly be considered unreasonable which asserted that Hauriou's schema, however suggestive at the time of its formulation, presents no little difficulty in the matter of its application to French constitutional history since the end of the Third Republic. Perhaps any comment on such a contention is in a measure doomed to futility. Concepts of historical periods, historical cycles, and the like

[3] In theory, the fact that the parliamentary system which prevailed from 1814 to 1848 was monarchical in character is irrelevant. However, inasmuch as in actuality republicanism as well as parliamentary government has become identified in France with political democracy, a schema of post-Revolution history in terms of republicanism is not unnaturally a possibility likewise. This has, as a matter of fact, been interestingly formulated by the late Charles Seignobos. See his *Histoire politique de l'Europe contemporaine* (7th ed.; Paris, 1929), I, 278 ff. A combination of the two patterns is not difficult to effect. Cf. J. T. Shotwell (ed.), *Governments of Continental Europe* (rev. ed.; New York, 1952), pp. 56 ff.

are, it may be agreed, fundamentally arbitrary in character. Hence their justification is to be found, if anywhere, in their convenience. If a particular suggestion is not felt to be an aid to thinking and to understanding, the simplest solution would seem to be to abandon it. On the other hand, the student of parliamentary government in France may feel that, in the presence of the almost insuperable difficulty of viewing in perspective events of which he is a contemporary witness, his most fruitful procedure is to make the most serious effort possible to detect some line of historical continuity.

Manifestly, Hauriou's conclusion that establishment of the parliamentary system of the Third Republic was "definitive" turned out to be, in the literal sense, incorrect. On the other hand, there may exist a perspective in which the conclusion need not necessarily be abandoned. Thus, the case would not seem wholly indefensible for the contention that the Vichy period is to be considered a largely irrelevant episode. On this view, the interlude can be dismissed as having been based on foreign armed force and thus essentially non-French. In turn, this hypothesis would lead to the conclusion that the Fourth Republic was primarily a continuation of the Third, both having the common characteristic of being the sort of democratic regime the French seem disposed to choose when they are free to choose. Indeed, the Fourth Republic, according to a development that was frequently remarked, tended in the course of its history to become more and more similar to the Third. This leaves De Gaulle and the Fifth Republic. For manifest reasons, they are exceedingly difficult to view in perspective.

The question is clearly not susceptible of precise answer how far the nice balance that is the ideal of parliamentary government may in practice oscillate in one direction or the other without, as a result, virtual disappearance of the system itself. Gaullist and kindred critics of the Fourth Republic persistently contended that the regime was so close to assembly government as to be in fact a stultification of parliamentary government. The Fifth Republic may be tentatively viewed as an aberration at least equally great in the opposite sense. In any case, it can scarcely claim to have a genuinely popular basis. The view is difficult to believe, and impossible to prove, that the Fifth Republic would have come into existence in the absence of actual and potential disloyalty in the armed forces. Subsequent appeals to the people hardly afforded them freedom of choice in a normal sense. The likelihood would seem to be that the future of the prevailing regime will encounter the problems inherent in any system built primarily around one man. If by good luck the disappearance of De Gaulle is followed by a relatively calm transition to another system, that system may well be situated on the "strange diagonal," in other words, characterized by a nicer equilibrium than that of either Fourth or Fifth Republic. In that event, the later political career of De Gaulle will possibly appear in history as substantially another interlude. The story according to which Cromwell, upon his incursion into the House of Commons, commanded, with reference to the mace, that "that bauble" should be taken away has been somewhere made the occasion for reflection concerning the contrast in respect of durability between the strong man and the kind of authority of which the mace remains a symbol. Some such repetition in history is not inconceivable. In any case, the teaching of earlier history will presumably continue to be relevant.

Parliamentary Government in France: Revolutionary Germs

Although the analysis according to which parliamentary government was introduced into France at the time of the

Restoration does not involve an unduly wide perspective, a slight shift to moderate emphasis on historical continuity serves to fill in a few not unimportant details. On this view, not only must assembly omnipotence and executive dictatorship be conceived as themselves resultants of development, but also, by the same token, traces of the origin of parliamentary government may be expected to appear in the course of each of the two processes.

The evolution of executive dictatorship in the first cycle may be thought of as beginning with the Directory and culminating in Napoleon as emperor. Moreover, although a full-blown imperial regime may properly be considered to be the antithesis of the parliamentary system, reason and experience suggest that where an autocrat feels constrained to recognize as running against him a strong current of popular forces, he will at least pay lip service to a political system that is characterized by conciliation, namely, to parliamentary government. In this context, the Additional Act may, with little or no forcing of the answer, be regarded as a written constitutional basis for a parliamentary empire.[4] Indeed, some essayist interested in historical speculation of an extremely hypothetical character might attempt an account of a possible parliamentary empire in Europe. The fate of the Additional Act if Waterloo had been less disastrous to Napoleon, the fate of the Liberal Empire and of its Constitution if the Franco-Prussian War had been avoided or had progressed favorably for France, the fate of Russia if Kerensky had been successful, and the fate of the Maximilian amendments to the German Imperial Constitution if

---

[4] John A. Hawgood, in his *Modern Constitutions since 1787* (New York, 1939), writes at p. 85, as if quoting an anonymous epigrammatist: "Louis XVIII played the Charte: Napoleon doubled and played the *Acte additionnel.*"

the attitude of the Allies and other conditions had been different would be some of the topics demanding treatment.

The evolution of assembly omnipotence is to be viewed as extending from the States-General to the Convention. Here again, reason would suggest that the most powerful legislature could scarcely expect to reduce the executive to a position so permanently subordinate that no signs of the parliamentary relationship would manifest themselves. Whatever may be said of an ingenious modern attempt to find at the time of the Convention the origin of parliamentary government in France,[5] there can be no doubt that clear signs of origin may be seen in the two years preceding the Constitution of 1791.

The familiar characterization of the French Charter of 1814 as *octroyée*, or "condescended," [6] involves considerations which are not without interest and importance in connection with the problem of parliamentary government. For one thing, the fiction that a national representative body owes its origin to an act of royal grace could be argued on historical grounds to form a better basis than abstract principles for the development of the concept of king-in-parliament, which in turn represents a highly favorable foundation for the evolution of the ministerial responsibility of the parliamentary system. Moreover, it is scarcely an accident that the Charter

[5] Reference is to B. Mirkine-Guetzévitch. Cf. his article in *Revue du droit public*, Oct., Nov., Dec., 1935, printed separately as *Le Parlementarisme sous la Convention nationale* (Paris, 1936), and his "Le Gouvernement parlementaire sous la Convention," in *Cahiers de la Révolution française*, no. VI, 1937, pp. 45–91. The case probably remains sufficiently doubtful not to injure seriously the claim of the Third Republic to being the first example in history of a parliamentary republic.

[6] The happy suggestion of finding a translation for a difficult word through reviving *condescend* as a transitive verb is apparently due to Hawgood. Cf. *op. cit.*, pp. 91 ff.

of 1814, being in theory the gift of the king, possessed the brevity and the generality that are conducive to constitutional development through flexible adaptation. The contrast here is with the elaborateness which writers such as Lowell and Bryce have underlined as characterizing more typical but less durable French constitutional documents, meticulously formulated with abstract principle as a foundation and logic and symmetry as imperatively required qualities. In this context, the Constitution of the Third Republic, the second of the two most important documents in the history of parliamentary government in France, may, without undue strain, be assimilated to the Charter of 1814. Although the provisions of 1875 were not literally *octroyées*, they were, in conditions that are well known, formulated by a monarchist majority in the hope and belief that they would be easily adaptable to the subsequent establishment of a monarchical regime. Brevity, generality, flexibility, and adaptability proved to be as important qualities for the development of parliamentary government under a republic as under a monarchy.

The possibility that Louis XVI might have "condescended" to France a constitution similar in character to the Charter of 1814 is, on the whole, far from a fanciful historical hypothesis. Indeed, it is the conclusion of a number of scholars, one of whom, for example, is of the opinion that before 1789 a charter like that of 1814 would have received the support of an "overwhelming majority" of the bourgeoisie and the clergy.[7] Another, it is not without interest to note, suggests that Madame de Staël was right in holding that the declaration proposed in June of 1789 by her father, Necker, was almost word for word the same as Louis XVIII's St.-Ouen

[7] Georges Lefebvre, *The Coming of the French Revolution*, tr. by R. R. Palmer (Princeton, 1947), p. 74.

declaration.[8] In any case, had such an event occurred, either before or reasonably soon after the meeting of the States-General in 1789, there can be little if any doubt that the course of French history would have been greatly smoother. Once the certainty became established that the Constituent Assembly was to formulate the elaborate kind of document to which Lowell and Bryce refer, conditions favorable to the development of parliamentary government became correspondingly remote. However, the Assembly, in the course of demonstrating how unfavorable a basis for parliamentary government an abstract, doctrinaire, and elaborately detailed constitutional document is, likewise furnished illustration of the fact that, in conditions which do not represent rigid limitations on relatively free growth, characteristics of the parliamentary system will display themselves almost as a matter of course.

French constituent bodies, the long line of which includes primarily the National Constituent Assembly of 1789-1791, the Convention of 1793, the National Assembly of 1848, the Bordeaux Assembly of 1871, and the two Constituent Assemblies of 1945-1946, are all alike, and differ from American constitutional conventions, in that they have served as basic governmental institutions of the country at the same time that they have been engaged in drafting a constitution for the future government of the nation. In other words, the members of such French assemblies have, in the course of exercising constituent authority, gained as well practical experience in the problem of governing. In the case of the Assembly of 1789-1791, performance of the dual function involved precisely the wide divergence between theory and practice which proved fatal to such germs of the parliamen-

[8] Emile Dard, *La Chute de la royauté* (Paris, 1950), p. 119.

tary system as appeared. This meant that the members of the Assembly practiced themselves and accepted in practice what they would not allow to be stated in cold print and what they thereby undertook to forbid to their successors. The causal considerations that were involved were naturally exceedingly complex. Not least important was the force of doctrinaire abstract principle. The outstanding examples are, of course, the concept of national sovereignty and the doctrine of the separation of powers.

The late G. K. Chesterton has somewhere suggested that we of the twentieth century are in some measure inferior to the men of the eighteenth century because we do not possess as they did the faculty of believing in abstract principles so sincerely as to inform them with an immediate and tangible reality. Insofar as this involves a tendency to draw unquestioned conclusions from unexamined premises, the virtue, whatever its elevated moral tone, is a doubtful one for purposes of clear thought and wise decision. The members of the Assembly of 1789–1791 not infrequently afforded grounds for this doubt.

I

King versus National Assembly:
A Problem Posed

THE several dates that may be suggested, and have been suggested, to mark the point at which royal absolutism came to an end in France all have one thing in common. They recognize that the end of the Old Regime was closely related with the meeting in 1789, for the first time in 175 years, of the States-General. Absolute monarchy, the assumption is, was at an end when there existed alongside the monarch a body which was in some sense representative of the nation.

The "Nation Represented"

The question of the date at which, in the earlier part of the reign of Louis XVI, the convening of the States-General became *morally* certain is, of course, far from simple. From the nature of the case, a specific date is much more difficult to determine than in ordinary instances. On more than one occasion, the king had hinted that he recognized the importance, and even the necessity, of periodic meetings of the representatives of the three Estates. More than one far-sighted minister had presented to the king arguments in favor of summoning these representatives. Liberal noble advisers had urged the step. The voice of the judiciary, that is to say, of the *parlements,* had uttered, for whatever motives, authoritative declarations to the same effect. These convictions and expressions were, of course, not only mutually influenced by one another; what is more important, they had their basic origin in the much-discussed conditions—political, financial, economic, and social—that existed in the France of the time. So far as the States-General are concerned, the simple fact is that their meeting was in some sense destined before formal announcement of their convocation was made.

When on 8 August 1788 the king, through an Order in Council, convened the States-General for the early part of the next year, the end of the Old Regime may be said at this point to have been decided. The student to whom this kind of date and this kind of event appeal may hold, with a distinguished French constitutional historian, that the king, at this time and by this act, brought about the Revolution.[1]

In summoning the States-General, the king may doubtless be said to have indicated an intention to re-establish the much discussed "Ancient Constitution of France." [2] However this may have been, the intention can in retrospect be seen to have been doomed to failure. History, especially that of England, suggests that a real solution of an emergency through invocation of old ways is possible only on certain conditions. The adaptation which the solution will require must mark merely a step in a relatively gradual development. In other words, the solution, though asserted to be based on a return to fundamentals, must in reality be progressive. Only thus will the paradox of a step forward by a step back-

[1] Maurice Deslandres, *Histoire constitutionnelle de la France de 1789 à 1870* (Paris, 1932), I, 33: "Et dès le mois d'août 1788 on peut dire que la Révolution est réalisée par le Roi lui-même."

[2] Cf. Bibliographical Note, p. 246.

ward fail to appear too violent. But, of course, such conditions did not exist in the France of 1788. After all, a period
of 175 years is a respectable span, and too much had happened for the meeting of the States-General that was summoned for 1789 to take place just as if such meetings had
regularly been held all along. More particularly, the Third
Estate could not in the circumstances be expected to be con-
tent with the position it had held nearly two centuries before.

The summoning of the States-General was a recognition
of the fact that reform was imperative. It was also a recognition of the fact that the king could not, without the col-
laboration of the nation, effect real reform. But the Third
Estate had come to be representative of the nation in a way
in which the two privileged orders were not. Hence issuance
of the Order in Council of 27 December 1788, by which the
Third Estate was allotted a number of representatives equal
to that of the other two orders combined, marks a date of
the first importance. The king's acceptance, however reluc-
tant, of the direction and force of public opinion aroused
high hopes in the country. With such acceptance nothing
but a single representation of the people, involving a pre-
ponderant position for the Third Estate, seemed consistent.

Though privilege could doubtless not have been expected
readily to accept the changed order of things, its resistance
was doomed to failure. Its opposition to the clear implications of the Order in Council did, of course, give rise later
to much difficulty, difficulty which would have to be resolved before the two elements, king and nation, could be
brought into a clear juxtaposition; but, even at the time, a
perspicacious observer could understand that the situation
presaged a joining—and reconciling—of the primordial issue
between the traditional and progressive points of view. In
January of 1789, such an observer wrote that the fundamental political issue had rapidly changed complexion, constitu-

tional limitation of absolutism having become secondary to recognition of the Third Estate as the real representative of the Nation.[3]

The delegates of the French nation could, like those of any nation, be said truly to be its representatives only on condition that they were free to attempt formulation of the views of the nation.[4] This consideration explains the importance of the date 24 January 1789, the day on which, it will be recalled, Louis XVI issued a letter directing *cahiers* of grievances to be drawn up and brought to the meeting of the States-General. Although, at the time of the discontinuance in 1614 of the States-General, *cahiers* had become a well-established feature of the meetings of the representatives of the orders, the king's letter in January of 1789 assumed especial significance. Either the gesture was empty and unmeaning, or else it was an invitation to basic reform. Politically, absolute monarchy was at an end.[5] Monarchy as a system was no doubt at the time endorsed, but it was new monarchy resting on new foundations and on recognized principles.[6]

[3] J. Mallet du Pan in his diary. See *Mémoires et correspondance de Mallet du Pan pour servir à l'histoire de la Révolution française,* ed. by A. Sayous (Paris, 1851), I, 163: "Le débat public a changé de face. Il ne s'agit plus que très secondairement du roi, du despotisme et de la constitution; c'est une guerre entre le tiers-état et les deux autres ordres, contre lesquels la cour a soulevé les villes."

[4] For a discriminating and provocative discussion of representation in connection with the French Revolution, cf. Marcel Prélot, *Les Institutions politiques françaises de 1789 à 1870* (Paris, 1951), pt. I, "La Monarchie révolutionnaire," pp. 37–43.

[5] Cf. A. Mathiez, *La Révolution française* (Paris, 1922), vol. I, "La chute de la royauté (1787–1792)," p. 46: "L'examen des cahiers montre que l'absolutisme était unanimement condamné."

[6] Thus, F.-A. Aulard, *Histoire politique da la Révolution francaise: Origines et développement de la démocratie et de la république (1789–1804)* (Paris, 1901), p. 30, writes: "Sans doute, les cahiers sont

Probably the most obvious specific day from which to date the end of the Old Regime in France is the day on which the States-General actually met, 5 May. From that date forward, the "nation represented" was a real fact. The form that such representation was destined eventually to take was, it is true, yet to be determined. Owing to resistance by the privileged orders and to the stand, however wavering, that was taken on their side by the king, influenced by the queen, by his brothers, and by the court, the situation remained for nearly two months uncertain. The time was consumed, as has been often narrated, by negotiations between the Third Estate on the one hand, which insisted on a meeting in one assembly, where the method of voting would involve the counting of individual deputies, and on the other hand the privileged orders, which stood out for three separate bodies, with separate voting by the orders. The issue, as has been argued with considerable cogency by various juristically minded writers, was indubitably one of legality versus illegality. At the same time, the representatives of the Third Estate, as was not unnatural in the circumstances, assumed an attitude which, though from a legalistic point of view somewhat highhanded, was not without its own logic. They could and did maintain that, if the contention of the privileged orders should be accepted, the doubling of their number was unmeaning and, even worse, disingenuous.

Neither the royal speech nor the ministerial speeches on 5 May presented a clear statement concerning the matter of meeting and voting. The privileged orders somewhat joy-

plus timides que les livres et les pamphlets; mais, généralement, on y réclame une Constitution, et une Constitution, c'était la fin de l'absolutisme; c'était, en partie, la Révolution." This is echoed by Deslandres, *op. cit.*, I, 39: "C'est la mort de la Monarchie absolue."

fully deduced from this fact the assumption that the "Ancient Constitution" was to prevail. On the other hand, the Third Estate argued that silence was an implicit recognition of changed conditions and of the primacy of the typical representatives of the nation. As a corollary of this argument, the Third Estate refused from the beginning to concern itself, as an order, with the credentials of its members. It naturally felt that to do so would be to accept the contention of the privileged orders. Consequently, it persistently insisted, in its negotiations with the other two Estates, that they should meet together with it. Finally, the Third Estate decided, on 10 June at the suggestion of Sieyès, to summon the privileged orders to a meeting that would have as its purpose the examination of credentials. At the same time, it asserted that, whether the Clergy and Nobles should accept the cordial summons or not, it would undertake the examination of credentials, not in its capacity as a separate order but on behalf of the States-General as a whole. This attitude may, from a juristic point of view, be accepted as having been in conflict with legality; by the same token the attitude was, literally speaking, revolutionary.

On 17 June, again at the suggestion of Sieyès, the Third Estate, with whom about twenty members of the Clergy had joined, took the momentous step of declaring itself to be the National Assembly of France. This was an overt act—definitely a first revolutionary act, and the day may thus appear, not merely to the juristically inclined, as the precise date on which the Revolution began.

On 17 June, again, the National Assembly, which the Third Estate had proclaimed itself to be, undertook to enact into law financial provisions not only of a statutory but even of a constitutional character. Then, three days later on 20 June, a date which may also be singled out as that on which the death knell of absolute monarchy sounded, the members of the National Assembly took the famous Tennis Court Oath, by which they swore not to separate until they had given France a constitution.[7] By this time, the vacillating king had determined to assert himself, but his speech of 23 June, in which he commanded separate meeting and voting on the part of the three Estates and in which he defined the limits within which he would assent to reform, was, whatever its merits in substance, ill-timed. The pronounced character of Louis XVI's unusual firmness served to cause his subsequent capitulation to appear by contrast only the more abject. The Third Estate immediately refused to obey, and, within a day or two, it received the support of more than half the members of the Clergy and of a small number of important Nobles.

On 27 June, only four days, that is, after his strong stand before the States-General, the king ordered the Clergy and the Nobles to meet with the Third Estate.[8] As the future mayor of Paris, Bailly, presiding officer at this time of the National Assembly, exclaimed, "This day renders the family complete." More than one well-known scholar is of the opinion that what was previously revolutionary thus became regularized by the king's command. The States-General had become in law as well as fact the National Assembly.

Whatever date may be selected as that at which the French Revolution began, the important thing for the study of parliamentary government is, it may be stressed, that at this time alongside the king a National Assembly came into a

[7] Only a handful of the clergy was present, and no representative of the nobility.

[8] Professor Crane Brinton, in his *A Decade of Revolution: 1789–1799* (New York, 1934), p. 5, contrasts the event with "the lurid affair of the Bastille."

No! Louis did not recognize the National Assembly till mid-August. To him the joint meetings were simply meetings of the States-General.

modern existence. The two elements, the king and the National Assembly, the one an ancient and traditional symbol of the country, the other its modern representation, the one a reflection of the unity, the other of the diverse composition of the nation, had to coexist if parliamentary government, which is essentially an attempted solution of the problem of the relationship between these elements, was to develop. In terms of abstract analysis, the existence of these two elements is not only manifestly necessary as a basis for parliamentary government; it is likewise sufficient. On the other hand, the historical connotations of the two elements are of paramount importance. If this is true of kingship, it is a consideration of even greater significance in connection with the representatives of the people.

Parliamentary government of course can, as it did for the first time in history during the Third Republic in France and as it has done there and elsewhere since, operate without a king. Theoretically indeed it can operate without any formal head of state at all. But it cannot, from the nature of the case, operate without representatives of the people. And though the existence of any legislative assembly raises, at least potentially, the question of the relationship of legislature and executive, not just any legislature can, in the context of historical connotation, be said to serve as a satisfactory element in the true parliamentary relationship. The legislative assembly must have assumed a form in which the assembly is felt really to be representative of the nation, and it must have acquired a position of authority such that final decision with respect to questions fundamental to the welfare of the nation belongs to the assembly. This is precisely what happened in France in 1789, within a few months after the meeting of the States-General. The National Assembly assumed such a form and acquired such a position. This is the reason why, in respect of the study of parliamentary government, so much importance attaches both to the events leading up to 27 June, in the course of which the States-General took on a national character, and to the events immediately following that date, in the course of which issue was joined between the National Assembly and the king and resolved in favor of the Assembly. Moreover, a most striking consideration deserves to be deeply underlined. The perspective in which these events in France are to be viewed is in a definite sense that of months, in contrast with the corresponding situation in England, where the perspective is in an equally definite sense that of centuries.

In England in the eighteenth century, the necessity came to exist, it seems clear, that a solution should be found for the problem of the relationship between king and Parliament, on the basis of the Glorious Revolution and of the Bill of Rights. But Parliament, it may be said, had assumed its characteristic form by the middle of the fourteenth century; and the issue between king and Parliament, even in its acute form, was contested throughout a century, the seventeenth, before being resolved in favor of Parliament. This contrast forms no small part of the explanation why, although the ultimate solutions in France and England were essentially the same, the two courses of development were in many respects dissimilar.

Revolution and Counterrevolution

When Louis XVI, on 27 June 1789, ordered the Clergy and the Nobles to join with the Third Estate in the National Assembly, a successful political revolution had, to all appearances, been peaceably effected. Apparently, all the National Assembly had to do was to perfect its organization—the work of a few days—and then to address itself to reforms, of which the foremost was the formulation of a constitution. In actuality, the National Assembly attempted to do just this. Thus, in the first week of July, initial steps were taken with a view to work on the Constitution.[9] On the other hand, the peaceable nature of the Revolution, characterized by regularization through royal assent of technically illegal acts on the part of the Assembly, was in large measure more apparent than real. The king, as is well known, did not sincerely accept the changed situation, and still less so did the queen, the king's brothers, and the court. In other words, counterrevolution was decided upon and attempted.

The initial step of the reactionary side was naturally to arrange a concentration of military force. The intention of directing this force against the National Assembly was so manifest that the Assembly was, equally naturally, alarmed, and directed its attention seriously to the situation. In other words, the National Assembly found itself at grips simultaneously with revolution and with counterrevolution. Hence any study of the activities that were undertaken by the Assembly at this time does not find itself concerned solely with events which were directly related to the problem of the framing of a future constitution for France. Such study finds itself at the same time concerned with indiscriminately intermingled events which were related to the royal reaction and to the crisis aroused by it in the country, especially in Paris. Of these events, only the constitutional developments, of course, are of direct concern to the study of government. Military and economic and social developments form the background.

[9] For the sources, cf. Bibliographical Note, pp. 243–245.

Constitutional First Steps

The National Assembly, on 6 July, arrived at a decision to establish a committee of thirty members [10] that would have as its function the preliminary study of questions connected with the formulation of the Constitution. By the next day the committee had been constituted. A majority of the members were "moderates," supporters, that is, of limited, orderly, political reform. This committee of thirty chose as its leader, to report on its behalf to the Assembly, Mounier, the young Grenoble lawyer who had in 1787 gained considerable prominence in his native province through successfully defying the king. Latterly, he had been the member of the National Assembly to propose the Tennis Court Oath.

Mounier presented his report on 9 July. The greater part of the document consisted of a general discussion of the nature and importance of a constitution, emphasis being laid on the obligation which was said to devolve on the National Assembly to furnish such a constitution to France. In the course of this discussion, Mounier posed, and answered in the negative, the significant question whether France already possessed a constitution. As might be imagined, the matter turned largely on the question of definition. Mounier, though acknowledging that France was not "entirely unprovided with all the fundamental laws suitable to form a constitution," argued that the very absence of definition and of definiteness permitted no other conclusion than that a constitution did not exist. "When the manner of governing does not derive from the will of the people clearly expressed, they have no constitution." The reporter, however, was not

[10] Chosen, according to a system long traditional in France, with one member in each of the sections (*bureaux*) into which the Assembly was by alphabetical rotation (later by lot) divided. Cf. pp. 27, 73.

inclined to insist at great length on an argument about words. Even those persons, said Mounier, who contended that France possessed a constitution recognized "the necessity of perfecting it, of completing it"; and, he added, "the aim is therefore the same." The report was concluded with a brief outline of the principal divisions of a draft constitution. This was arranged under ten headings, beginning with a Declaration of the Rights of Man.

The report of the preliminary committee of thirty on the Constitution, in the course of its somewhat general discussion and of its somewhat vague proposals, had the merit of causing to stand out in clear relief the two elements, king and nation, which it was the principal problem of the Constitution to bring into a satisfactory working relationship. This is the principal interest that the report has for the study of parliamentary government. The problem was clearly presented. The parliamentary system was, it is easy to see, a possible solution, and was, almost certainly, a desirable solution.

One remark which was made by Mounier in the course of his report is of no little importance in connection with the history of parliamentary government. "It must be confessed," he said, "that in France lack of a constitution has not been, up to the present day, favorable to the Crown. Often audacious ministers have abused its authority." This initial Revolutionary instance of a traditional hostility in France to ministers [11] was to be followed from time to time by other examples.

The connection is manifest between French hostility to

[11] Reference may be made to E. Lavisse, *Histoire de France illustrée depuis les origines jusqu'à la Révolution*, vol. IX, "Louis XVI (1774–1789)," by H. Carré, P. Sagnac, and E. Lavisse (Paris, 1911), pp. 402, 405, 408.

ministers and the position of a king above criticism. In this fundamental sense, ministerial responsibility would seem to be inherent in a developed monarchical system. A historical sketch of the phenomenon would lead far, but a few passages culled from Bodin are of more than passing interest. He writes:

Doubtless, there is much to be said in favor of the King's ruling directly, but weighty reasons on the other side prevail over these advantages. . . . The safest maxim that a prince can follow is this: to be loved by all and hated by none. Now this means that the King must stand above all disputes. . . . He ought to be loved by all his subjects and looked up to by all as a high and sure fortress. . . . The state cannot fail to prosper when the sovereign holds to what pertains to his majesty, when the council guards its authority, when the magistrates execute their authority, and when justice takes its regular course.

In other words, "the sovereign will be well advised to let his ministers govern." [12]

Mounier, in his report, deplored the principle of absolute monarchy as being "necessarily arbitrary," but he went on to assert that concentration in the monarch of "authority without bounds" did not render the king personally responsible for the inevitable abuses of that authority. Actual examples, he felt, were particularly striking where they took the form of cases in which good and enlightened intentions of a monarch, moved by a desire to further the national happiness, were defeated, as the report suggested, by "obstacles" interposed by ministers acting on behalf of "the pretensions of privilege."

[12] This is the summarization of Bodin's position in W. T. Jones, "Machiavelli to Bentham," in *Masters of Political Thought* (Boston, 1947), II, 70–71, from which is taken, with the kind permission of Houghton Mifflin Co., the translation quoted.

The distinction in respect of responsibility between a king and his ministers has, it need scarcely be pointed out, been of paramount importance in the history of parliamentary government. The concept of an absolute king without blame, of a king who "can do no wrong" legally or morally, is "a working hypothesis" of the greatest convenience and utility. It symbolizes, with all the clarity resulting from personification in terms of a single, individual, human leader, the principle of the illimitable legal authority which must exist in every state, tempered and softened by the ideal which holds that such authority should be exercised only within the limits defined by the principles of absolute goodness and rightness and justice. This concept of a perfect relationship of law and morality is of so much moment as an ideal that its symbol ought in principle to be left untouchable. The manifest practical difficulties can be taken care of through institutional arrangements which will ensure that exercise, as distinguished from possession, of authority shall rest in the hands of persons, namely, ministers, who can be held responsible for actual shortcomings. Indeed, an obligation exists to effect these practical arrangements, whatever may be their apparent flaws in logic and symmetry—an obligation that is binding in a degree commensurate with the importance of the symbol of a perfect relationship. Had the National Assembly, in spite of everything, refrained from the attempt directly to limit the royal authority and confined itself to grappling with the problem in an indirect fashion through concern with the position of the ministers, it is not too much to say that the history of France in general and the history of parliamentary government in that country in particular would have been vastly different from what they have been.

II

Confidence and the Prerogative of Appointment and Removal

THE report which was read on 9 July 1789 to the National Assembly by Mounier on behalf of the committee of thirty was ordered by the Assembly to be printed, and a decision was taken that matters dealt with in the report should be discussed in the thirty *bureaux*. Two days later, on 11 July, the Assembly, in spite of distractions that were being caused by counterrevolutionary activities, more especially by the critical events resulting from the threat of armed forces, undertook to begin a discussion of the Constitution. The immediate occasion for the discussion was a proposal made by Lafayette. The committee of thirty had, it will be remembered, placed at the head of its topical outline the matter of a Declaration of the Rights of Man. It was to this question that Lafayette addressed himself. He supported in a brief speech the utility of a declaration of abstract principles, hoping to initiate a useful discussion of them by offering a tentative sketch of such a declaration. This was the beginning of a series of somewhat sporadic discussions of a famous subject, discussions that culminated in definite action only some weeks later.[1] The debate, abstract in its terms and largely academic in character, is for the most part of little direct interest to the study of parliamentary government. Meanwhile, however, a well-known event took place that does seriously concern such study. This was the dismissal by Louis XVI of his Director-General of Finance, Necker, and of three other ministers. The event occurred on 11 July, the day on which Lafayette had introduced his proposal.

The Debate (13 July) on the Dismissal of the Ministers

By obtaining the dismissal of Necker, the reactionary advisers of the king in their counterrevolutionary activities pushed matters beyond the threatened attack through force on the representatives of the nation. These advisers made a direct attack on ministers who possessed the confidence of the nation and of its representatives. Whether these ministers deserved the regard in which they were held, whether, for example, Necker's reputation was, as has been generally concluded, greater than his genuine merits warranted,[2] need not be considered here. The important thing is that public opinion clearly and vigorously approved the ministers. Dismissal of them was the immediate cause of the series of outbreaks with which has come to be associated all the meaning of the national holiday, 14 July, anniversary of the capture of the Bastille.[3]

---

[1] On 27 August. Cf. Ch. III, p. 76.

[2] Reference may be made, somewhat at random, to F. Funck-Brentano, *La Révolution française* (Paris, 1935), p. 7: "Necker était évidemment un financier averti; mais il n'avait rien d'un homme d'état."

[3] Reference may be made to Jean-Albert Bede, "Le Quatorze juillet et sa fortune littéraire (1789–1902)," in *Cahiers d'histoire de la Révolution française*, 1947, no. 1, pp. 91–109.

In 1789, 12 July was a Sunday. As a consequence, the National Assembly was not in session. However, soon after the convening of the Assembly on Monday the thirteenth, a member arose and announced the dismissal of Necker and the other ministers, news that must have been known to everyone present. The announcement gave rise to a long and somewhat confused discussion, from the course of which the records of several highly interesting speeches are preserved.

In an opening speech, Mounier analyzed the situation. He proposed a deputation and an address to the king which would, among other things, ask the recall of the ministers, assert the Assembly's lack of confidence in the existing advisers of the king, and point out the dangers inherent in the change of ministers. The speech and proposal are reported as throwing the Assembly into great disorder, in the midst of which a number of members, including a representative of Paris, Target, an Academician who at the time enjoyed considerable reputation as a lawyer, proposed various expedients for coping with the situation. Finally, the liberal noble, Lally-Tollendal, another Academician and representative of Paris, gained a hearing. In a long and eloquent speech, followed by loud applause, he supported the position taken by Mounier. He expressed the fear that an effort to secure the recall of Necker would not obtain any immediate results, but he favored formulation by the Assembly of an expression of thanks and of esteem in connection with the Director-General of Finance and the other ministers. Two other liberal nobles, Clermont-Tonnerre, representative of Paris, and the Comte de Virieu, from Dauphiné, followed with speeches that were in substantial agreement with those of Mounier and Lally-Tollendal.

The long speeches and the variety of proposals presented

to the National Assembly following announcement of the dismissal of Necker served to throw the Assembly into still greater confusion. No decision seemed possible. Petitions arrived from Paris, and dispatches were read which related what was going on in that city. Proposals to the effect that a deputation be sent to Paris were added to those that favored a deputation to the king. Other speeches followed. Finally, matters were brought to a head by the arrival of a messenger from the commandant of Paris, who communicated an alarming account of conditions in the capital. The Assembly, after recovering from the first effects of this shock, decided upon two deputations, the first to proceed to the king and the second to convey the reply of the king, if satisfactory, to Paris.

After an interval, the deputation that had been sent to the king returned. The president of the Assembly gave to that body an account of the representations which he had made to the king. Repeating to the Assembly his insistence to the king on the alarming situation in which the country found itself and on the necessity of altering the military arrangements, he continued: "I added that the National Assembly recognized the right that His Majesty had to determine the composition of his Council, but that it could not conceal from him that the change of ministers was the primary cause of the existing misfortunes." The reply of the king, as reported by the President, was far from satisfactory. The king asserted that his views were already known and that he alone would decide what further measures, if any, were necessary. No mention was made by him of the ministers. The Assembly, again aroused, found difficulty once more in deciding upon any of the suggestions that were put before it. Finally, a proposal was passed stipulating that a committee be chosen to frame a resolution. This action was taken, and the resolution as presented was subsequently adopted unanimously. The wording of the resolution, in such parts as dealt directly with the ministers, was as follows:

The Assembly, interpreter for the nation, declares that M. Necker, as well as the other ministers who have just been dismissed, carry with them its esteem and regrets. . . .

Declares that ministers and civil and military agents in authority are responsible for every undertaking contrary to the rights of the nation and to the decrees of this Assembly.

Declares that the present ministers and the advisers of His Majesty, of whatever rank and estate they may be, or whatever functions they may have, are personally responsible for the present misfortunes and for all those that may ensue. . . .

And the present determination shall be communicated to the king by the president of the Assembly and published in printed form.

The Assembly further resolves that the president shall write to M. Necker and to the other ministers who were dismissed to inform them of the decision which concerns them.

The resolution was not presented to the king until the following morning. He informed the president that he would examine its terms. The Assembly, having decided that its sitting should be continuous and having chosen Lafayette vice-president, in order that an overtaxed president might have relief, suspended its sitting shortly before midnight.

The conditions in which the National Assembly found itself at grips with the characteristic feature of parliamentary government, that is to say, with ministerial responsibility, were, it seems clear, scarcely the most favorable for a discussion of so important a concept. As a matter of fact, formulation in words of the concept of responsibility manifestly requires no small amount of nicety and subtlety of expression. Ministerial responsibility involves indubitably a relationship in which principle is much modified by fact. Therefore, the relationship must be considered as a combination of certain quantities of theory and practice. These quantities will naturally vary in a measure with circumstances; and, in the midst of crisis, the balance will inevitably tilt somewhat toward fact and practice.

Experience suggests that expression of a concept in which theory and practice are combined is likely in considerable measure to assume the form of paradox. Hence formulation of the expression will not infrequently take the form of a balanced sentence. Such a sentence will normally present a simple structure: in theory and in principle, such and such will be asserted to be the case; *but,* in practice, facts, it will be contended, require modifications that are thus and so.

So far as ministerial responsibility and, more particularly, appointment and removal under the parliamentary system are concerned, the nature of the concept is simple enough. In principle, the decision is that of the king; in practice, the *final determination* is that of the people and their representatives. However, within the outlines of this structure, considerable variation is possible. As may easily be imagined, the famous French flair for clarity of expression can find in this possibility of variation an opportunity worthy of its serious effort. Basically, the principal variation will result from difference of emphasis. This difference of emphasis, in turn, is most simply effected by weighting that side of the balance which is last expressed. Thus, a difference is manifest between the proposition that, whereas the king has in principle the decision, the legislature exerts the practical influence and the proposition that, whereas the legislature has practical influence, the king has the decision.

On the fateful thirteenth of July of 1789, the balance of theory and practice which was involved in the relationship of ministers to king and of Assembly through ministers to king was, in the course of discussion, definitely tilted, because of the crisis existing and of the emotions aroused, in the direction of practice, in the direction, that is to say, of assertion of the actual authority of the Assembly. In the debate, the principal speakers, as supporters of the monarchical system of government, maintained a correct attitude toward the king and expressed high regard for his exalted position and his prerogative; *but,* as liberals, they had their last word for, and hence they placed their emphasis on, the authority of the nation and its representatives.

So far as the king's side of the balance was concerned, the expressions which were employed in the debate on 13 July could scarcely be criticized by anyone as being understatements. Indeed, the language which was used was so forthright as to serve to cause the paradoxes which were formulated to appear, in any logical context, unnecessarily violent. For example, not only did Mounier and Target stress the principle that the king had "the right" to appoint and to change his ministers; the Comte de Virieu insisted on recognition of "the right inherent in the Crown for the king to appoint the ministers, agents of his power." And, whereas Clermont-Tonnerre proclaimed that "the king is master" in the matter of constituting his Council, the eloquent Lally-Tollendal asserted that "the king is absolute master in constituting his Council as he pleases." At the same time, all these speakers, having recognized the theoretical position of the king, went on vigorously to denounce dismissal of Necker and the other ministers.

Although the proposition that the king possessed "the inherent right" to dismiss his ministers and that he was "absolute master" in doing so would seem logically to preclude intrusion of any other authority in the matter, the speakers probably felt that the very vigor of their language and the resulting violence of their paradoxes served to indicate the real strength of the sentiment which moved them to insist on the paramountcy of the nation and its representatives. Just what these representatives could and should in the circumstances do was, from the nature of the case, less clear and certain. Proposals were not lacking, but it is distinctly doubtful whether their implications were at the time fully understood.

The least bold suggestion which was made to the National Assembly on 13 July advocated insertion into the minutes of a statement setting out the attitude of the Assembly. Such a statement would express regret on the part of the Assembly concerning the dismissal of Necker and of the other ministers and would assert further that communications to the Assembly had arrived from various sections of the country expressing thanks to the dismissed ministers and, in some cases, going so far as to demand their return. Just above this sort of suggestion in degree of boldness were proposals that favored incorporating expression of the same kind of views in an address to the king, proposals, in other words, to the effect that the king should be informed of the feelings of the nation and its representatives, but that no recommendations should be made. Thus, for example, the Comte de Virieu, though he advocated an address which would contain a tribute to the recent ministers and which would present to the king "a picture of the truth" painted with "strokes of fire," was yet not willing that specific recommendations should be made. "I do not think," he said, "that we ought to undertake to embarrass exercise of the king's legitimate power by designating to him the ministers that he ought to take. This would be to lend a new arm to the calumny that accuses us to the king. It would be said that we wish in some sort to lay our hand on his scepter. It ought never to be possible to reproach us with having infringed on a single one of the principles that we recognize."

Views like those of the Comte de Virieu involve, it would seem, a somewhat curious, and moreover a somewhat misplaced, distinction. Insofar as the National Assembly possessed authority with respect to the composition of the king's Ministry, this authority was, according to general agreement, primarily that of influence through opinion. In order for opinion of the nation and of its representatives to be influential, it had to be brought to bear on the king. In order for it to affect the king, views had to be formulated in such a way that they would be sufficiently clear to the king. Hence there can be little doubt that an address to the king setting out the views of the Assembly was superior to insertion in the minutes of an expression of such views. Moreover, inasmuch as the Assembly had definite opinions concerning who should be and who should not be the king's ministers, a definite obligation rested upon it, in expressing its views, to express them clearly and fully. Whether or not the king would agree with these views, how far, in other words, he might be influenced by the opinion expressed, was another matter. That, it would seem, is where the real distinction lay. The National Assembly could not itself appoint or dismiss ministers; it could perfectly legitimately tell the king that, in its opinion, he should take such action. If the king should accept the opinion of the Assembly, the distinction would in a given case be, practically speaking, very thin; but the distinction would in principle nonetheless remain.

Such considerations go a long way toward defining the concepts of "confidence" and "lack of confidence," concepts that have been so intimately connected with the development of parliamentary government. Indeed, this connection was clearly recognized by the ablest speakers taking part in the debate in the National Assembly on 13 July. When the Comte de Virieu objected to "designating" the ministers to the king, either he meant that the Assembly ought not to appoint the ministers, something that no one suggested it should, or else he meant that the Assembly, in setting out its views, ought not to express its opinion on who the ministers should be, a scruple that would result in a suppression of opinion with respect to the most definite aspect of the question at issue. On the other hand, other speakers were on sounder ground. Thus, Clermont-Tonnerre was restrained but firm. "The nation," he said, "ought not to appoint the ministers; it can only indicate them through evidence of its confidence or of its disapproval." Target was even more definite:

Opinion ought to direct the executive power. That is the truth which ought to be conveyed to the prince. Let us with firmness make clear to him the evil which force does to itself in replacing men who had the public confidence by men who never can get and ought never to get it.

The same sentiment and attitude stood out through the eloquent words of Lally-Tollendal. After denominating the king "absolute master" in constituting his Council, he continued:

We can indicate to him good servants, as we can turn him from bad. We can address to him respectful, tender, submissive prayers. We can say to him that there are circumstances in which the virtue of a prince does not suffice by itself alone, in which it has need to find the assistance of other virtues in his Council, and that we are assuredly in one of those circumstances. We can conjure him by the love we bear for him, by the fidelity we shall always maintain toward him, by the entrails of our torn native land, to recall the only ministers worthy of his confidence and the only ones who possess ours.

And yet none of these expressions made any substantial additions to the resolution of Mounier, which had inaugurated the debate, or to the speech in which the Grenoble lawyer supported his resolution. Thus, Mounier had asserted:

The National Assembly ought to enlighten the monarch. It ought to request the recall of the ministers, victims of their devotion to the interests of the throne and to those of our native land. Through gratitude, through love of justice, it ought to make clear to the king the dangers to which France is exposed and to declare to him that the National Assembly can accord no confidence to the ministers who by remaining in office, or to those who by accepting the functions of MM. Necker, de Montmorin, de la Luzerne, and St. Priest, manifested principles contrary to the public good.

The Fall of the Bastille

On 14 July the National Assembly convened for a morning sitting at nine o'clock. The proceedings were relatively calm. Various items of routine business were dispatched, and two debates of more than passing interest took place. Thus, in the latter respect, a long discussion was held of Lafayette's resolution that a Declaration of Rights be placed at the head of the Constitution. Some speakers supported this proposal, whereas others argued that such a declaration ought to be placed at the end. In the result, the only consensus which was realized took the form of a simple decision that a declaration should be included in the Constitution. In the second place, an extended discussion arose concerning what plan of procedure should be followed in connection with work on the Constitution. The final decision in this matter was, after consideration of various proposals, in favor of a committee of eight members [4] to draft a Constitution which would be discussed in the *bureaux* and, on the basis of this discussion, debated in the Assembly.

An afternoon sitting on the fourteenth, beginning at five o'clock, opened with the resumption of a discussion concerning the acute problem of troop concentration at Versailles. The keen debate was dramatically interrupted by the appearance before the Assembly of one of the first nobles to join with the Third Estate, the young Vicomte de Noailles, representative of Nemours. He announced to the Assembly the happenings of the day in Paris, and more especially the capture of the Bastille. This news at first completely disrupted discussion in the Assembly. After a short time, a decision was arrived at to send a deputation, accompanied by the Vicomte de Noailles, to the king. In the interval, discussion in the Assembly, which had been resumed as in keeping with the dignity of that body, was again interrupted by the arrival of a deputation from Paris, which announced further distressing news of the capital. A second deputation to the king was decided upon, but before it had departed the first deputation returned. The second deputation waited only long enough to hear the short and unsatisfactory reply of the king and then departed. During their absence, further news arrived from Paris. Soon afterward, the second deputation to the king returned with another unsatisfactory reply. The Assembly decided to send a third deputation the following morning. Thereupon it drafted a message to be sent to Paris and suspended its sitting at two o'clock in the morning.

At a morning sitting on 15 July, the National Assembly

[4] Those chosen were Mounier, the Bishop of Autun (Talleyrand), Sieyès, Clermont-Tonnere, Lally-Tollendal, the Archbishop of Bordeaux (Champion de Cicé), Le Chapelier, and Bergasse.

further directed its attention to the question of sending another deputation to the king, as it had late the night before determined to do. Several members proposed an address to the king, whereupon a distinguished naval officer representing Reims, the Marquis de Sillery, read to the Assembly an address of considerable length which he had already prepared. This proposal asserted that the time had come for frank speaking. It insisted that the king had been "deceived"; and suggestion was made that the king would profit if there should be sketched for him an account of "the perfidious counsels his ministers dared to give him." In addition to this statement of grievances, the proposed address asserted that had the king listened to the Assembly, the massacres of the day before would possibly have been avoided. Then it continued: "There is still perhaps a way to calm the irritated people. Your Majesty knows those who have given him these perfidious counsels. Remove from you, Sire, these public pests." Finally, the suggestion was made that if the means proposed should fail to restore calm, the king should come into the Assembly.

The reading by the Marquis de Sillery of his draft of an address, though it was said to have made a strong impression on the Assembly, gave rise to long and somewhat disordered discussions. In the result, the address was not brought to a vote, the Assembly unanimously deciding merely to send a deputation to the king with certain instructions. After the members of the deputation had been chosen, they were on the point of departing when announcement was made that Louis XVI had on his own initiative decided to come before the Assembly. This news was received with acclaim.

After a short delay, the king appeared. He was without guards, being accompanied only by his two brothers. He advanced into the Assembly; and, standing, he delivered a short speech, constantly interrupted by applause, in which he expressed confidence that the king and the assembly of representatives of the nation would, mutually relying one on the other, solve the difficulties which existed. At the end, the king announced that he had ordered withdrawal of the troops.

The president of the Assembly replied to the king's speech. After thanking the king, the president communicated to him, on behalf of the assembly, certain decisions of that body. He concluded as follows: "Finally, it renews its representations to Your Majesty concerning the changes effected in the composition of your Council. These changes are one of the principal causes of the disastrous troubles that afflict us and that have torn the heart of Your Majesty." Louis XVI replied in a few words; and, though he expressed his approval in respect of two or three particular matters, he made no comment on the president's remarks concerning the ministers. The king thereupon withdrew and proceeded on foot to the Château, accompanied by the members of the Assembly amid scenes of great enthusiasm.

When the Assembly later reconvened, its deputation to Paris was sent off at once. Thereupon, one of the famous "Triumvirate," Barnave, Mounier's young lawyer colleague from Grenoble, introduced a motion with a view to bringing about dismissal of the present ministers "as not deserving the confidence of the people and being absolutely unworthy of it." He argued that the citizens of Paris would presently be demanding the removal of the ministers and that the Assembly ought to anticipate such an eventuality, in order that its dignity should not be compromised through an appearance of acting under the influence of popular clamor. Mirabeau, whose failure to take part earlier in the discussions growing out of the dismissal of Necker was apparently due to absence from the Assembly because of the death of his father on

12 July,[5] strongly supported Barnave's motion; but Clermont-Tonnerre prevailed on the Assembly to postpone its decision. Clermont-Tonnerre disclaimed eloquently any intention of defending the ministers, in whose denunciation he joined; but he argued that on a day so fine the king should be left undisturbed in his happiness, and the Assembly should be too conscious of its dignity "to concern itself with so vile a Ministry."

The Aftermath of 14 July

The National Assembly opened proceedings at its sitting on 16 July in an atmosphere reflecting the momentous events that had taken place in Paris. Announcement was made that Lafayette was in Paris, where he had been appointed colonel general of the bourgeois militia. President Bailly appeared before the loudly sympathetic Assembly and announced that he had been chosen mayor of Paris. Mounier read a long and detailed account of the activities of the deputation that had been sent to Paris on the previous day. In this account, assertion was made that "in all the streets of Paris, as in the assembly-room of the City Hall, dismissal of the new ministers and the return of M. Necker were loudly demanded"; and a striking paragraph told of an eloquent speech that became famous, made by Lally-Tollendal at the City Hall. Following the reading of Mounier's recital in the Assembly, Lally-Tollendal was urged to repeat the speech. This he did. Upon its conclusion, he added:

That is the speech I thought it my duty to deliver. I spoke in the name of the Assembly. If I received applause, it was offered only as homage to this body. I shall add that there was

[5] Criticism of the great orator and accusations of cowardice directed at him are met by his Swiss friend, Etienne Dumont, in *Souvenirs sur Mirabeau et sur les deux premières Assemblées législatives* (Paris, 1832), p. 116.

only one cry at the City Hall, in the City Hall Square, indeed in the whole city—demand for the dismissal of the ministers and for the return of the virtuous man who is now removed from the court and who has so well served our native land— in other words, M. Necker. I could not conceal from you the wish of the capital, because my fellow citizens begged and conjured me to place it before you.

When Lally-Tollendal had finished his speech, Mirabeau arose to present a draft proposal of an address to the king. This initiated another debate on ministerial responsibility. Mirabeau supported his proposal in a speech in which he demanded dismissal of the ministers. The address contained expressions of respect and loyalty toward the king, a long indictment of the ministers, and the assertion that the Assembly could have no confidence in them. Then, in his conclusion, Mirabeau put a rhetorical question which suggests that he possessed a remarkable feeling for the fundamental nature of parliamentary government. He seems clearly to have understood that this system, operating through ministerial responsibility, involves in essence a harmonious relationship between executive and legislature, resting on the people as a basis. "Will the nation believe," he asked, "that harmony is perfect between Your Majesty and ourselves if the Ministry is suspect, if it is regarded as the enemy of our labors?" Finally, the draft address concluded with the familiar balanced sentence, this time phrased by the great Mirabeau:

We in no wise pretend to dictate the choice of your ministers; they ought to be pleasing to you; to be pleasing to your heart is a condition necessary for them to serve you: but, Sire, when you consider the disastrous course on which your counselors wished to cause you to embark, when you reflect on the discontent in the capital, a capital to which they laid siege in a desire to starve it, when you reflect on the blood that they caused to flow, on the horrors that can be imputed to them alone—all Europe will find you indulgent if you deign to pardon them.

Mirabeau's draft address to the king met with wide approval in the Assembly. After all, it merely advised dismissal of the ministers, a step that had for some time seemed to represent the desire of the Assembly. No mention, it is true, was made of Necker, and the suggestion has of course been made that Mirabeau, owing to personal hostility to Necker, deliberately omitted from his draft proposal demand for his recall. In any event, what seems to have been a spontaneous demand arose in the Assembly that the address should go further and advocate Necker's recall. This step received practically unanimous support, and yet a few important opponents constituted interesting exceptions. In fact, but for this opposition it seems likely that no debate would have taken place. In the event, Mounier, who thereby reversed his position of three days before, Barnave, and Clermont-Tonnerre spoke against the action proposed. The tone of their remarks and the careful lawyerlike analysis which they employed indicate that conditions had changed since the debate of 13 July. Emotions that had been aroused by the dismissal of the ministers had with the passing of time cooled, and the situation had undoubtedly been affected in a measure by such events as the appearance of the king in the Assembly and the withdrawal of the troops. Of the occurrence of this change, the altered position of Mounier was particularly strong evidence. In any event, the debate clearly proceeded in a calmer atmosphere and on a higher plane of reason.

Barnave's opposition to Mirabeau's proposal followed upon the reading of the draft address and upon amendment

of it as proposed by acclamation. The words of the young
Grenoble attorney are of no little interest:

Although it is in principle true that the Assembly has not the
right to ask the dismissal of a minister or the recall of another,
it is no less true however that, when a minister has not the confidence either of the nation or of its representatives, the National Assembly can and should declare that it will not correspond with him concerning the affairs of the realm, and then
the dismissal of such a minister becomes necessary. But the
situation is not the same in the case of the recall of a minister
who has been removed, because, for the same reason that the
National Assembly cannot be forced to correspond with a royal
counselor whom it does not esteem, the king cannot be constrained to take back the minister who has succeeded in displeas-
ing him. I think that the return of M. Necker cannot be asked,
and that action must be confined to expressing in this regard
the desire of the National Assembly and that of the city of
Paris, so loudly proclaimed in so terrible a manner.

The contentions of Barnave, it may be suggested, displayed some of the characteristics or hairsplitting. In principle, his position, it is true, was not only clear but plausible.
The basic concept of harmony between king and Assembly,
harmony, that is, between executive and legislature, is, in
connection with parliamentary government, well recognized
to be sound. That ministers should possess the confidence of
both the king and the Assembly seems a not unreasonable
deduction from that concept. Furthermore, a distinction on
this basis between recommendation by the Assembly of the
dismissal of certain ministers and insistence by the Assembly
on the recall of certain ministers is certainly comprehensible.
Dismissal can be supported on the grounds of lack of confidence on the part of the legislature. Recall can be opposed
on the grounds of lack of confidence on the part of the execu-

tive. Ministers definitely agreeable to both legislature and executive are at least conceivable. In practice, however, the situation is not the same. At the time that Barnave was speaking, more than one example could have been cited from English history of ministers appointed by a king who considered them not only objectionable but detestable.[6] This is to say that, in general, force of circumstances and the logic of events had shown themselves stronger than the king and than the logic of abstract principles.

Confidence in the ministers is, it may be reiterated, a fundamental concept of parliamentary government; but underlying even so basic a concept is the fact that, under the parliamentary system, final authority rests in substance with the legislature and with the voters. Hence such confidence in ministers as may be felt by the formal executive is secondary to the confidence felt by the legislature and the voters. In fact, the harmony between executive and legislature which characterizes parliamentary government is a harmony that results precisely from the confidence which is felt in the ministers by the legislature. If harmony exists, if, that is to say, the legislature has confidence in the ministers, the system works. On the opposite hypothesis, the system ceases to work until harmony is re-established, until, that is to say, ministers and legislature are again in general agreement, a situation which must be effected either through different ministers or through a different legislature. In either eventuality, the ministers must have the confidence of the legislature. The formal executive is, practically speaking, in some sense an onlooker. More particularly, if circumstances are such that only one minister or one group of ministers can command the confidence of the

[6] On the subject, reference may be made to George Burton Adams, *Constitutional History of England* (rev. ed.; New York, 1934), ch. xvi.

legislature, the formal executive must acquiesce, no matter what his personal feelings may be. Discretion on the part of the formal executive disappears. The question of his confidence becomes almost wholly irrelevant. Barnave's distinction breaks down. Indeed, at this time the recall, a day or two later, of Necker by the king was to show the relentless working of the force of circumstances. This was in France the more striking in that no developed parliamentary system existed. On the other hand, it is not surprising in the circumstances that Barnave failed to understand that his distinction was a highly theoretical one. In practice, French kings had been for too long possessed of real power for the idea at once to become prevalent that the king, in so important a matter as the choosing of his ministers, might on occasion possess no discretion.

Even at the present day, of course, the question of the degree of discretion possessed by the formal executive in choosing ministers, in choosing in practice, that is to say, the prime minister, cannot be said to be susceptible of any very precise and final answer. A situation closely analogous to that which prevailed in France in 1789 is practically impossible to imagine. The dismissal and the recall of ministers, in the sense in which these matters were at that time discussed, are today scarcely conceivable. On the other hand, that some discretion may on occasion exist, however complex may be the problem of locating its limits, would seem to be generally accepted.

No small part of the difficulty of exact formulation grows out of the fact that, on an occasion where discretion on the part of the formal executive appears to exist, action by the formal executive may be presumed to have some influence on the attitude of the legislature, whereas the amount of such influence has a definite bearing on a judgment of how much discretion the formal executive had in the beginning. Thus, in the much discussed case in England in 1923, the king, George V, is usually agreed to have been possessed, in respect of the successor of Bonar Law, of a possibility of choice which was not merely perfunctory. Circumstances pointed, with considerably less certainty than is normally the case, to who the next prime minister would be. The king's action in sending for Stanley Baldwin is commonly regarded as having been eminently sound. Certain it is that Baldwin proved to have the confidence of the majority in the House of Commons, proved, that is to say, to be acceptable as leader of the Conservative Party; but how much this eventuality was due to the fact that the king's choice had fallen on Baldwin it seems impossible confidently to say.[7] So also, had the king sent for Lord Curzon, no human mind can claim actually to know whether or not he would have become the recognized leader of his party.

In the period since establishment of the Third Republic, the president of the French Republic has frequently, according to the usual accounts, been possessed of real discretion in the matter of choice of the prime minister. When the president, after his conventional consultations and his analysis of the situation, sends for a given leader, who asks time to canvass conditions, and when such a leader later declines on the ground that he has been unable to secure the support of a majority, the president, it may be said, is proved to have made a mistaken use of his discretion. The same is true when a leader accepts the president's invitation, only to prove unacceptable to a majority on appearance before the Assembly.

[7] A striking recent analysis of the situation is to be found in R. T. McKenzie, *British Political Parties: The Distribution of Power within the Conservative and Labour Parties* (New York, 1955), pp. 39–41.

Insofar as choice by the president exerts influence and thus confers an initial advantage, such influence and advantage are in the two hypotheses manifestly not sufficient. In spite of the influence and the advantage, the president's discretion is proved to extend less far than he imagined. In other words, what appears to be an exercise of discretion is not in reality so. On the other hand, if a leader succeeds in securing the support of a majority of the Assembly, this would seem by no means to prove that another leader could not, if invited, have obtained approval by a majority. This is merely to say that under the parliamentary system discretion in the matter undoubtedly exists but that its limits are impossible accurately to determine.

When, on 16 July 1789, Barnave had concluded his remarks in opposition to Mirabeau's proposed draft of an address to the king, announcement was made of the resignation of the Minister of Paris and of the Royal Household, Villedeuil, one of the ministers in office at the time of the convening of the States-General who had not been removed at the time of the dismissal of Necker. This resignation was a presage of future developments in the practical situation; but, at the time, the president of the Assembly observed that the news would have no effect on the proceedings in progress. As a consequence, discussion of Mirabeau's proposal was presently resumed.

Mounier, as has been said, presented an argument that contrasted strikingly with the position he had taken in initiating the debate that had followed announcement of Necker's dismissal. He now contended that for the Assembly to refuse its confidence to ministers was, though "indirect," none the less an encroachment on the king's prerogative and therefore a violation of sound principle. Acceptance of such practice would, he said, result in intrigues in connection with the constitution of ministries; and, though Mounier was one of the "moderate" members known as Anglophiles, he invoked in this respect what he alleged to be the great abuses that prevailed in the English Parliament. He therefore opposed all action except suggestion to the king that Necker be recalled, and he asserted that this was proper only because the king, at the time of his appearance before the Assembly, had specifically asked the advice of that body concerning steps to be taken in the existing situation. Barnave, who had favored suggesting dismissal but opposed demanding recall of the ministers, intervened again merely to point out that in any free nation an assembly would exercise influence on the composition of a ministry and that such influence involved "inviting" the king to dismiss the ministers, not "exacting" of him their dismissal. Thereupon, Mirabeau, in a long and eloquent speech, supported the action that was proposed and answered the several points made by Mounier. The latter replied, repeating briefly his opposition to interference with the royal power. He went so far as to assert that, until the Constitution should be adopted, it was "not in keeping with the dignity of the nation to have influence on the choice of ministers." Mirabeau, in turn, refraining from entering into the merits of the question of interference by the Assembly with the royal power, confined himself to asserting that "it is certain that the nation has the right to control the use which the ministers make of the royal authority." After a deputy, holding that all were in agreement but were unable to find a suitable formula, had offered as his contribution "not asking the dismissal of the ministers" as against "denouncing them," Clermont-Tonnerre spoke mildly in opposition to Mirabeau's draft address, suggesting that the king was already well acquainted with the attitude of the Assembly and that he would doubtless of himself carry out that body's wishes. The debate was brought to an end through an eloquent appeal that was made by Lally-Tollendal. On all sides, he held, public opinion was crying out in demand for the recall of Necker. This, he continued, constituted an order addressed to the Assembly. His views succeeded in uniting the members, a decision being arrived at to send a deputation to the king to ask the dismissal of the ministers and the recall of Necker.

The exchange between Mounier and Mirabeau, in the course of the debate of 16 July 1789 on the proposed address to the king, shows Mirabeau at his best. In one of the most effective of all the great orator's speeches, he showed a grasp that was in the circumstances nothing short of remarkable of what have come to be regarded as the basic principles of parliamentary government. He made to each of the points developed by Mounier what must appear to be a devastating answer.

Mounier had on 13 July phrased in conventional paradoxical form the relationship between king and ministers, in order to stress, in the emotional situation that at the time existed, the practical side of the balance; that is to say, he had insisted that *in fact* the influence of the Assembly transcended the *principle* of the king's authority. Thus, he had said:

Certainly the king has the right to change his ministers; but, in this moment of crisis, would not the representatives of the nation betray their every duty if they did not warn the monarch of the dangers to which impudent counselors do not fear to hand over the whole of France?

On 16 July he showed what a difference change in emphasis can make. Now the stress was on principle. In the result, the distinction between theory and fact became so much less important as practically to disappear. "To refuse," he said, "its confidence to a minister to whom the king has given his would be on the part of the National Assembly an indirect way of obliging the king to dismiss him." Mounier, on 13 July, had advocated demanding of the king precisely such a dismissal. Three days later he found an expression of no confidence in ministers to be "a blow to the liberty and power" of the king.

To Mounier's argument Mirabeau replied in terms of the very nature of ministerial responsibility. He had already, in his draft proposal, recognized that this responsibility must be expressed through a paradox in which the balance is weighted on the side of the fact of the power of the people. "We in no wise pretend," he had written, "to dictate the choice of your ministers, but . . ." and so on. And then, in his speech, he paid his respects directly to Mounier's present opposition to the exercise of any influence by the National Assembly.

If there is an ungodly and detestable maxim, it is that which would forbid the National Assembly to declare to the monarch that his people have no confidence in his ministers. This view is an attack at the same time on the nature of things, on the essential rights of the people, and on the law of ministerial responsibility—law that we are charged to enact, law even more important, if that is possible, to the king than to the people, law which will never be in free use unless the representatives of the people have, if I may be permitted so to express myself, the initiative of accusation.

The famous orator concluded this part of his argument with an eloquent period:

Ah! Since when do the approval and the disapproval of the people no longer constitute a judgment as between good and bad ministers? Why should a nation that is under a representative system exhaust itself in vain murmurs, in sterile imprecations, rather than cause to be heard the wish of all through its attested organs? Has not the people placed the throne between heaven and itself, in order to realize, so far as men can, eternal justice, and at least to reveal its decrees for the happiness of this world?

When Mounier expressed opposition to the exercise of any influence on the king by the National Assembly on the ground that this would constitute encroachment on the prerogatives of the king, he invoked what has been called "one of the most famous dogmas of modern political evangelism," [8] the doctrine of the separation of powers. At the time the famous principle was, as both Mounier and Mirabeau recognized, soon to receive serious attention at the hands of the Assembly, in connection with discussion of the Constitution and of the Declaration of the Rights of Man. Upon this principle Mounier based his opposition to the proposed address to the king. "Commingling of the powers," he said, "must be prevented; the National Assembly must not confuse the executive and the legislative power."

The principle of the separation of powers was often to be invoked by the National Assembly, just as it has continued to be invoked down to the present day. Whatever in the end may be said concerning a doctrine which has undoubtedly proved highly controversial, which certainly involves no inconsiderable elements of vagueness, obscurity, and difficulty, and which has been interpreted and applied differently in different countries, modern students whose attitude toward the doctrine is not altogether one of reverence will find Mirabeau's remarks in his reply to Mounier of no small interest:

We shall soon have occasion to examine this theory of the three powers, which, exactly analyzed, will perhaps show the

[8] By the distinguished professor of public law, the late Gaston Jèze. See his *Les Principes généraux du droit administratif* (Paris, 1904), p. 125.

facility of the human mind to take words for things and formulas for arguments, and to direct itself toward a certain realm of ideas, without ever turning back to examine a definition which, because intelligible, is taken for an axiom. The valorous champions of the *three powers* will then try to make us comprehend what they understand by this great locution of *three powers*, and, for example, how they conceive the judicial power to be distinct from the executive power, or even the legislative power to be without any part in the executive power.

He continued:

It suffices for me today to say to them: you forget that this people to whom you oppose the limits of the three powers is the source of all the powers, and that it alone can delegate them. You forget it is with the sovereign power that you dispute control over administrators. In fine, you forget that we, the representatives of the sovereign, we, before whom are suspended all powers, even those of the head of the nation, if he does not proceed in agreement with us—you forget that we do not pretend by means of our decrees either to appoint or to remove the ministers, but only to reflect the opinion of our constituents concerning such or such minister.

Mounier, on the other hand, was on ground on which had stood framers of recent American constitutions. In state and federal constitutions, the doctrine of the separation of powers had been applied in such a way as to establish a nonparliamentary relationship between legislature and executive. Legal responsibility of the executive was arranged, not political responsibility. As an instrument of control, impeachment was established, instead of harmony founded on confidence between legislature and executive, maintained by such things as criticism, control, resignation, and dissolution, which, experience shows, render employment of impeachment unnecessary and useless.

Mounier probably foresaw that American views, accord-

ing to which the parliamentary system, with its political responsibility of ministers, is commonly said to be the negation
of the doctrine of the separation of powers, would be applied
in the Constitution of France, soon to be formulated. This is
perhaps what he had in mind when he said that "at the time
the Constitution is framed, limits sacred to each of the powers
will be laid down," and when he held that "meanwhile" the
king should be left uninfluenced by the Assembly. Certain it
is, as will be presently seen,[9] "ministerial responsibility"
meant at the time to all but an enlightened few legal, not
political, responsibility; and impeachment was the constitutional means envisaged. And yet not the least remarkable
thing about the remarkable speech by Mirabeau is that it
demonstrated definitely that Mirabeau clearly apprehended
the important distinction between legal and political responsibility.[10] Hence he was able effectively to accuse of inconsistency an advocate of the doctrine of the separation of
powers who, while opposing an address to the king, accepted
impeachment.

Ah! How can you refuse us this simple right of declaration,
you who accord us that of accusing them, of prosecuting them,
of creating the tribunal that will undertake to punish these
artisans of iniquities whose works you, by a palpable contra-
diction, proposed to us to contemplate in a respectful silence?
Do you not see how much better lot I offer than you do to
the agents of government, how much more moderate I am?
You admit no middle ground between a dismal silence and a
sanguinary denunciation. And I? I warn before denouncing;
I challenge before blasting; I, before treating ineffectiveness

[9] Cf. Ch. III, pp. 81–83.

[10] Professor Chevallier goes so far as to say that Mirabeau was the
"only one" who could distinguish political and legal responsibility.
Cf. J. J. Chevallier, "The Failure of Mirabeau's Political Ideas,"
Review of Politics, XIII (Jan., 1951), 95.

and incompetence as crimes,[11] offer retirement. Which of us has more moderation and equity?

If Mounier could with apparent plausibility object to Mirabeau's draft proposal of an address to the king, on the ground that such an address would encroach on the prerogative of the king, and if he could found on the doctrine of the separation of powers his objection to this alleged encroachment, he was, it might be thought, still under some obligation to suggest practical reasons why the doctrine of the separation of powers should in the circumstances be a determining factor. On this point he argued that violation of the separation of legislative and executive powers would give rise to intrigue, and he cited England as an example. Thus, recognition of even an indirect authority on the part of the National Assembly to influence the composition of the king's Ministry would, he said,

give rise in it to a multitude of intrigues calculated to make one's enemies in the Ministry fall and to have oneself put in it; that is one of the greatest abuses of the Parliament in England, and one of the causes that bring most of the storms, whether in the Constitution or in the Ministry.[12]

[11] It is perhaps not without interest to recall the following passages from The Grand Remonstrance, 1641: "198. It may often fall out that the Commons may have just cause to take exceptions at some men for being councillors, and yet not charge those men with crimes, for there be grounds of diffidence which lie not in proof. 199. There are others, which though they may be proved, yet are not legally criminal." Cf. Samuel Rawson Gardiner, *The Constitutional Documents of the Puritan Revolution, 1625–1660* (3d ed., rev.; Oxford, 1906), p. 231.

[12] The short account in the *Moniteur* of Mounier's speech gives no adequate idea of his argument, which has largely to be inferred from Mirabeau's answer to it. The collection of Buchez and Roux (*Histoire parlementaire de la Révolution française* [Paris, 1834]) has no account at all. For a critical analysis of the sources, cf.

Mirabeau on this occasion showed no hesitation in taking up the cudgels for England. He began with irony. "England is lost!" he exclaimed. "Ah! Great Lord! What sinister news! . . . But what earthquake, what convulsion of nature has engulfed that famous isle, that inexhaustible source of such great examples, that classic land of the friends of liberty?" But he felt that there was reason to be reassured. "England," he said, "still flourishes for the eternal education of the world . . . and only just recently has she filled a great gap in her constitution, with all the most energetic vigor of youth and the imposing maturity of a grown up people in public affairs."

When Mounier had spoken of "intrigues" in England, he had apparently had especially in mind the situation in Parliament some six or seven years before and, more particularly, the dissolution at that time of the House of Commons by George III on the advice of the younger William Pitt. In any event, this was the situation that Mirabeau felt called upon to deal with. "You were then," he said, "thinking merely of a few parliamentary dissensions (there, as elsewhere, there often exists only idle talk which has scarcely any importance beyond the interest of loquacity); or rather it is apparently the last dissolution of Parliament that frightens us." Mounier, according to Mirabeau, had seen in a series of maneuverings in Parliament, followed by dissolution by the king, nothing but evil, the consequence of violation of the doctrine of the separation of powers. Mirabeau outspokenly attributed this to Mounier's inadequate understanding of English history and institutions:

I shall not say to you that, on your own showing, it is evident that you are unaware of the causes and of the details of that

J. J. Chevallier, *Mirabeau: un grand destin manqué* (Paris, 1947), pp. 67–68.

great event, which is in no wise a revolution, as you call it; but I shall say to you that that example offers the most irresistible proof that the influence of a national assembly on the ministers can never be disastrous, because it is nul, this influence, as soon as the senate abuses it.

If Mounier did not clearly understand the real character of dissolution, this ought in no way to be surprising. Very few people in France—and, it may be surmised, even in England —had at that time a thorough understanding of parliamentary government or, consequently, of the part played in it by dissolution. Indeed, even in recent times there has undoubtedly been in France a considerable amount of misapprehension concerning dissolution. Reputable French students of government have, it is true, been practically unanimous in considering dissolution an integral part of the parliamentary system in its true form. So also, in practical politics, some champions of political democracy have argued that dissolution is the only satisfactory method of referring to the voters a conflict between legislature and executive.[13] On the other hand, the single dissolution under the Third Republic came unfortunately to possess associations of a *coup d'état*; [14] and considerations of practical politics have been responsible for the fact that elements which are otherwise traditionally

[13] This was true, e.g., of Léon Blum and the Unified Socialists. Cf. Joseph Barthélemy, *Valeur de la liberté et adaptation de la République* (Paris, 1935), p. 201.

[14] There can be little doubt that MacMahon seriously considered a *coup d'état* at the time of the *seize mai* incident in 1877. Cf., e.g., E. Lavisse, *Histoire de France contemporaine depuis la Révolution jusqu'à la paix de 1919*, vol. VIII, "L'Evolution de la 3e République" by C. Seignobos (Paris, 1921), pp. 39 ff. In addition to this, the situation was, of course, complicated under the Third Republic by the constitutional stipulation (*Loi du 25 février 1875, relative à l'organisation des Pouvoirs publics*, Art. 5) requiring that the executive obtain consent of the Senate in order to employ dissolution.

champions of political democracy have consciously misrepresented the nature of dissolution by raising the bogey of dictatorship.[15] And, most fundamental of all, the influence of the concept of national sovereignty remains strong.[16]

In view of the modern situation as well as of the situation in 1789, Mirabeau's clear grasp of the real character of dissolution was the more remarkable.

What really happened in that unusual case in which the King of England, supported by a very weak minority, did not fear to combat the formidable national assembly and to dissolve it? Suddenly the fantastic edifice of a colossal opposition collapsed on its frail foundations, on that greedy and factious coalition which seemed to threaten to invade everything. Well! What was the cause of so sudden a change? It was that the people were of the opinion of the king and not of that of the parliament.[17] The head of the nation subdued the legislative aristocracy by a simple appeal to the people, to that people which never has but one interest, because the public welfare is essentially its own. Its representatives, clothed with an invisible force and almost with a veritable dictatorship when they are the organs of the general will, are only impotent pygmies if they are to substitute for their sacred mission interested views or particular passions. Therefore, let us give ourselves over without fear to the impulsion of public opinion. Far from fearing it, let us invoke ceaselessly this universal control. It is the incorruptible sentinel of our country. It is the first auxiliary instrument of every good

[15] Thus, the Radicals, modern Jacobins, have regularly shown themselves to be opposed fundamentally to employment of dissolution.

[16] For an interesting comment on this aspect of the matter, see R. Redslob, *Le Régime parlementaire* (Paris, 1924), pp. 195-197.

[17] Mirabeau naturally does not allude to what the situation would have been if the people had not been of the opinion of the king. For an interesting modern discussion of this matter, reference may be made to Sir Ivor Jennings, *Cabinet Government* (2d ed.; Cambridge, 1951), pp. 374-381.

constitution. It is the sole guardian, the lone and powerful compensator of every vicious constitution. It is the sacred guarantor of social peace, with which no individual, no interest, no consideration can be comparable.[18]

When the National Assembly was, on 16 July 1789, on the point of proceeding to a vote on Mirabeau's proposal, announcement was made that all the ministers had been dismissed. A resolution was immediately passed, stipulating that a deputation should be sent to the king to express to him the thanks of the Assembly.

Dismissal of the ministers by the king was, in view of the circumstances that prevailed, a culmination which is of the highest interest to the history of parliamentary government. The essence of the matter is exceedingly simple. In the absence of an established parliamentary system and even in the absence of any real tradition for such a system, the principles of the operation of the system manifested themselves in practice through the working of what may perhaps, without undue exaggeration, be regarded as inexorable natural forces. A distinguished French historian of representative government has suggested that the practice of ministerial responsibility preceded understanding of it.[19]

[18] What Mirabeau could not have known was that this was to be the last example of dismissal of a government by the king. At least this is the judgment of Sir Ivor Jennings (*loc. cit.*) who definitely rules out the case of Melbourne. For a good brief account of the younger Pitt's ministry, reference may be made to Alpheus Todd, *On Parliamentary Government in England: Its Origin, Development, and Practical Working* (2d ed.; London, 1887), I, 116–119, and to G. B. Adams, *op. cit.*, pp. 407–408. Adams suggests that Pitt's victory rendered impossible another like it.

[19] P. Duvergier de Hauranne, *Histoire du gouvernement parlementaire en France, 1814–1848* (Paris, 1857–1869), I, 96: "Le principe de la responsabilité politique se trouvait pratiqué avant d'être reconnu ou compris."

III

A Constitution for France:

Beginnings

SOLUTION in favor of the National Assembly of the critical situation of July 1789 growing out of the dismissal of Necker by the king naturally did not bring *ipso facto* calm and peace. At the same time, the king's action, representing at least for the moment acceptance of the underlying principle of parliamentary government, had effects that were indubitably reassuring. The same thing is substantially true of the visit which the king made to Paris on 17 July. From various parts of the country communications came to the National Assembly expressing gratitude for what that body had accomplished. The Assembly itself, in its deliberate and somewhat disorganized manner,[1] had of necessity to deal with numerous and varied details. These details were largely unrelated to one another, but they were immediately connected in a general way with the existing crisis. Although

[1] For the situation in this respect under the Constituent Assembly, see R. Bonnard, *Les Règlements des assemblées législatives de la France depuis 1789* (Paris, 1926), pp. 10–12. Cf. E. Lavisse and A. Rambaud, *Histoire générale du IVe siècle à nos jours* (Paris, 1896), vol. VIII, "La Révolution française, 1789–1799," pp. 106–108.

some uncertainty and disagreement not unnaturally existed in the Assembly concerning practical steps to be taken with respect to specific critical events, a general consensus prevailed that the way fundamentally to allay unrest was to proceed with a Constitution for France.

The Committee on the Constitution

The eight members of the Committee on the Constitution who had been chosen on 14 July had inevitably been much concerned with the fateful events of that day and the following two or three days. Consequently, once the initial hectic events had in some measure sunk into the background, the members were in a position to concern themselves with the Constitution. On 24 July a member arose in the National Assembly to propose that the committee should present at once some report on its work. This proposal received immediate support from other members of the Assembly, whereupon the Assembly decreed that on the following Monday, 27 July, the committee should give an account of its deliberations, stipulating further that the committee should by the same date reduce some part of its proposals to a form which would be susceptible of discussion. Meanwhile, on 21 July, the president of the National Assembly had undertaken to set in motion in the Assembly the arrangements necessary to prepare the way for discussion of the future basic law of France. Two days later, on 23 July, the subject of the Constitution again received attention when the National Assembly had occasion to issue a proclamation of some importance. The Assembly, as a result of continued reports of specific disorders, had decided upon an appeal to the country, "inviting" the people to peace. In the course of the proclamation, reference was made to the recent dismissal of the ministers, and stress was laid on the harmony that currently prevailed between the king and the Assembly. Finally, the proclamation asserted: "The National Assembly will concern itself, and will not cease to concern itself, with the great objective, the Constitution."

Promptly on 27 July, the Committee on the Constitution complied with the wishes of the National Assembly as expressed in the decree of 24 July. The Archbishop of Bordeaux, Champion de Cicé, read to the Assembly a report which set out on behalf of the committee the results of its deliberations until that time. The report stated, among other things, that the members of the committee had felt their first duty to be regard for the wishes of their constituents. With this object in view, the committee had begun by examining such *cahiers* as they had been able to consult. Clermont-Tonnerre, it was announced, would present in a special report to the Assembly an account of the general tenor of these *cahiers*. The report went on to say that, on behalf of the committee, Mounier would lay before the Assembly a draft of a Declaration of Rights and a draft of a first chapter of the projected Constitution. This first chapter, it was stated, would deal with the general principles of French government. These two additional reports, greeted like the first with vigorous applause, were duly read to the Assembly. In short, the National Assembly received on 27 July three reports concerned with the future governmental system of France.

The initial report of the Committee on the Constitution, read to the Assembly by the Archbishop of Bordeaux, requires no extended examination in connection with the study of parliamentary government. A few introductory paragraphs stressed the importance of the Constitution. A general expectation was recognized to exist throughout the country that the Constitution would be established and that through its establishment greater order and contentment would be realized. The main body of the report consisted of general comment on the subjects treated in the two supplementary reports which were announced—on the one hand, the *cahiers* and, on the other, the Declaration of Rights and the general principles of French government. Mention of the last of these three subjects led to the concluding paragraphs of the initial report. Reports on the structure of government would, it was stated, be presented without delay. Meanwhile, discussion of general principles would aid in perfecting the provisions of the Constitution. Members of the Assembly were invited to inform the committee of their ideas concerning the structure of government, more especially concerning that of the legislative branch. Still more particularly, their views were requested on two specific questions connected with the legislature. The first question was whether the legislative body should have a continuous existence, as the committee unanimously favored, or whether, as a large number of *cahiers* assumed, it should, as in the past, be brought into existence only from time to time. The second question was the fundamental one of structure—whether the legislature should be unicameral or should consist of two or more houses.

Recognition by the Committee on the Constitution that its first duty was to have regard for views expressed in the *cahiers* would appear to have been, in the circumstances, wholly natural. Formulation of expressions of grievances had historically become definitely associated with meetings of the States-General. Following the long period subsequent to the last meeting of the States in 1614, the command by Louis XVI that *cahiers* should be prepared was, in existing conditions, a particularly striking event. The greatest interest attended their formulation. Their contents, it seems certain, served as important evidence of prevailing public opinion. At all events, the fact is that the members of the

National Assembly indubitably considered that they ought to look upon the *cahiers* as guides. Imperative mandates, it is true, had early in the second week of July been held by the Assembly to be without binding effect,[2] but this did not prevent the *cahiers* from exerting marked influence. Indeed, such a conclusion is sufficiently established by the very fact that Clermont-Tonnerre's report of 27 July was regarded as desirable.

The text of the report on the *cahiers*, as read by Clermont-Tonnerre to the National Assembly, reflects careful, fair, and able study on the part of the author. The object of the study, it was stated, was to collect and to present the "light" that was to be found in the *cahiers*. The report, aside from a few introductory considerations concerned with the attitude of the *cahiers* toward the basic matter of establishment of a constitution, falls into two parts. One of these dealt with principles upon which there was general agreement, and the other with "questions on which the *cahiers* as a whole did not explain themselves in a uniform manner." These principles and questions were discussed in the body of the report, and they were concisely enumerated at the end. The principles that were held to be generally accepted were eleven in number, the questions of the second category eighteen. Of these latter, it may be said that though they dealt with details of no little importance, only a few were immediately related to the operation of parliamentary government. These exceptions had to do with summoning, proroguing, and dissolving the States-General. Some *cahiers* thought that these functions

---

[2] This principle, it will be recalled, was subsequently incorporated in the Constitution of 1791. See Titre III, Ch. I, Sec. iii, Art. 7: "Les représentants nommés dans les départements ne seront pas représentants d'un département particulier, mais de la Nation entière, et il ne pourra leur être donné aucun mandat."

belonged to the king, with the proviso that new summons should follow dissolution; others held that the States-General alone possessed the power of dissolution. So far as the eleven agreed principles are concerned, they may be easily classified. The last two of them were declarations of the sacred character of property and of individual liberty respectively. The first recognized that French government was monarchical in character. Of the others, four had to do with the position of the king. They were worded as follows: "II. The person of the king is inviolable and sacred; III. His crown is hereditary from male to male; IV. The king is the depository of the executive power; VI. The royal sanction is necessary for the promulgation of laws." On the side of the legislature, the following principles were enunciated: "VII. The nation makes law with royal sanction; VIII. National consent is necessary for borrowing and taxation; IX. Taxation can be agreed to only from one meeting of the States-General to another." Finally, one principle, which was asserted to be generally accepted, is of paramount interest and importance in connection with parliamentary government. "V. The agents of authority are responsible."

In the body of the report by Clermont-Tonnerre, the principle of responsibility was not discussed. There was merely the simple statement that "the responsibility of all agents of authority is demanded generally." As a matter of fact, even the most cursory examination of any considerable number of *cahiers* [3] will bear out the assertion made in the report. The two generalizations concerning ministerial responsibility contained in the report of Clermont-Tonnerre were based on several hundred expressions of the principle.

[3] Several hundred are readily accessible in Volumes I–VI of the *Archives parlementaires*. Volume VII is an index to the six volumes. Cf. Bibliographical Note, p. 244, below.

Many of the *cahiers* were as laconic as the report in the matter. The briefest statement that was employed was to be found where a *cahier* merely enumerated the demands on which the deputies who were concerned were to insist. In all cases, "The Responsibility of Ministers" was included in the list. Many *cahiers* contented themselves with demanding the same thing in only a few more words. Others, dealing with a certain number of details, were less concise in their phraseology; and some contained detailed expressions many times as long as the shorter statements. Altogether, there was an abundantly rich variety of terminology, though there was likewise some exceedingly striking similarity, and even identity, of phraseology. In some instances, the ministers alone were mentioned; in others, the ministers were included among other "agents of authority." Those *cahiers* which treated ministerial responsibility at greater length than did others expressly blamed past evils on ministers of the king, formidable requisitories being drawn up in some cases. As was natural, the king was in no instance criticized adversely. The ministers were in large numbers of cases declared to be "accountable," this word probably occurring as frequently as "responsible." In many instances, both expressions were applied to the ministers. According to prevailing terminology, accountability was apparently then as now generally associated with financial activities, responsibility with non-financial; but, in a few instances, this usage was reversed, the ministers being declared responsible in respect of finance and accountable in respect of general administration. The expression most often used in connection with accountability was "for the employment of funds" entrusted to ministers. However, variations in terminology with respect to financial responsibility occurred with considerable frequency. Responsibility was said variously to be for ministerial "management," "administration," "conduct," "authority," and the like.

There can be little doubt but that the accountability and responsibility envisaged in the cahiers were legal, not political, in character. Some *cahiers*, in speaking of ministerial responsibility, demanded that it be a "fundamental law" of the realm or of the state. The legal arrangement which was desired was undoubtedly that which had been developed in England. The common law principle that "the king can do no wrong" was tacitly accepted. Ministerial responsibility was demanded as a means of securing legal liability on the part of royal agents. Interestingly enough, recognition was given to the important corollary which had been developed in England, namely, that no minister could plead command of the king.[4] Thus, in France one *cahier*, in demanding responsibility made reference to such offenses as would involve violation of law and as would give rise to judicial action. In this respect, phrases like "infraction of the law" or "infractions of the laws" constantly occurred, and the idea of "guilt" and of "punishment" was frequently repeated.

Insistence on financial accountability was, it may be noted, entirely consistent with prevailing concepts of legal responsibility. Emphasis on the power of the purse proceeded from sound instinct, for this power is at the basis of both political and legal responsibility. Both governmental policy and governmental activity are translatable, and both are translated,

[4] The principle, it will be recalled, is incorporated in the Constitution of 1791. See Titre III, Ch. II, Sec. iv, Art. 6: "En aucun cas, l'ordre du Roi, verbal ou par écrit, ne peut soustraire un ministre à la responsabilité." In England, the principle, as applied to impeachment, had of course been incorporated in the Act of Settlement, 1701. For the situation in England, reference may be made to A. V. Dicey, *Introduction to the Study of the Law of the Constitution* (9th ed.; London, 1939), pp. 24–26, 325–327.

into the language of money. Control of financial programs involves control of policy, whereas control of accounts, though previous knowledge that it will operate serves in some measure as political control, is essentially a control which makes possible recognition after the fact of illegal action. This latter was the kind of action, as many *cahiers* make abundantly clear, to which financial "accountability" had reference. The same thing was true of the numerous demands made in the *cahiers* that financial accounts should be made public through printing. Information concerning governmental activities of all kinds is an indispensable means under parliamentary government for maintaining day-by-day political control over the executive, but publication of financial accounts serves, of course, as was contemplated in 1789 it would serve, to furnish information on which judgment may be based concerning the legality of ministerial action.

Likewise, in connection with the kind of responsibility that is not immediately related to finance, the responsibility that was envisaged in the *cahiers* was clearly legal responsibility. The simple demand that the ministers should be held responsible for their conduct cannot, it is true, be proved, in the absence of other considerations, not to refer to political responsibility. Neither, on the other hand, can it be proved not to refer to legal responsibility, and other considerations in great abundance indicate that this is precisely what was envisaged. Thus, in a slightly longer statement of ministerial responsibility, "violation of the laws" was expressly associated with "conduct"; and one of the most frequently repeated expressions in the matter demanded responsibility of the ministers for their "conduct in everything that is relative to the laws of the realm." So also, where mention was made of that most familiar expression of parliamentary government, namely, of "confidence," violation of it was spoken of as involving "punishment." Finally, responsibility of ministers was repeatedly recognized in the *cahiers* to involve judicial process. Action by established tribunals was frequently mentioned. Even where responsibility was declared, as it was in several cases, to be "to the nation," the States-General were clearly meant. In this respect, the expression "assembled nation" was several times employed; and in the many instances in which responsibility was explicitly said to be to the States-General, the intention was, as was indicated either expressly or implicitly, that the States-General should designate a court or should itself become a court for the purpose. This last-mentioned situation is to be regarded as typical. In other words, ministerial responsibility meant legal responsibility, and the procedure envisaged was either identical with, or corresponded in a general way to, impeachment. The conclusion would probably be too extreme that no single person connected with preparation of the *cahiers* had any concept of the distinction between legal and political responsibility; [5] the undoubted fact is that the *cahiers* clearly indicated the prevailing concept of ministerial responsibility to be a concept of legal responsibility. This merely renders the more remarkable the clear understanding which Mirabeau and a few others had of the distinction.

When, on 27 July, Clermont-Tonnerre had completed his

[5] For example, some interest attaches to the following passage (Art. 9) of the *cahier* for the Paroisse Chelles, La Prévôté de Paris hors les murs: "Le Roi nommera, comme à l'ordinaire, tous les ministres. . . . Mais chacun de ces ministres seront comptables aux Etats généraux de leur gestion, et en cas d'incapacité, de mauvaise administration, l'incapable ou le mauvais administrateur, sur la représentation des Etats généraux ou de la commission intermédiaire, sera renvoyé et le Roi supplié d'en nommer un autre" (*Arch. parl.*, IV, 425).

report on the *cahiers*, Mounier immediately proceeded to read to the National Assembly the draft that the Archbishop of Bordeaux had announced of a first portion of the Constitution. Mounier accompanied his reading with no report or other commentary, the earlier report by the Archbishop of Bordeaux doubtless being regarded as having served this purpose. The draft presented by Mounier consisted of two chapters. The first was entitled "Declaration of the Rights of Man and of the Citizen" and was composed of twenty-three articles. Chapter II had as its title "Principles of French Government," the chapter consisting of thirty-five articles.

The two chapters of draft constitutional articles that were read by Mounier are primarily of interest only as an indication of the views of the Committee on the Constitution and as evidence of what this committee conceived to be the attitude of the nation. Whatever may be their interest and importance to students of constitutional history, such interest and importance are distinctly secondary to the interest and importance of the discussions to which the articles gave rise and of the articles which were subsequently adopted by the National Assembly. In the Constitution that was destined to prevail, the Mounier draft is, except for a few scattered articles and except for the fact that a declaration of rights stands at the head of the Constitution, scarcely recognizable. So far as the study of parliamentary government is concerned, importance attaches to only a few of the Mounier articles.

The draft of the declaration of rights read by Mounier to the National Assembly on behalf of the Committee on the Constitution was, it can scarcely be doubted, more logical, more carefully phrased, and more symmetrical than the famous Declaration that subsequently succeeded in gaining acceptance by the Assembly. More particularly, the draft articles, unlike the articles ultimately adopted, were concerned with *rights* in the usually accepted sense of the word. The principal, if not the only, exception was an article that undertook to phrase the famous principle of the separation of powers. Inasmuch as this principle was to continue to be invoked as justification of the failure on the part of the National Assembly to accept important elements of parliamentary government, its inclusion at this time in a declaration of *rights* is of more than passing interest. The draft Article XIV was couched in the following terms: "In order to avoid despotism and to assure the reign of law, the legislative, executive, and judicial powers ought to be distinct. Combination of them in the same hands would put their possessors above all law and would permit them to substitute their wills for it."

The second chapter of the committee draft constitution, the chapter on the principles of French government, naturally contained a larger number of articles relevant to the problem of parliamentary government. More specifically, among thirty-five articles that were devoted to the basic aspects of a system of government, some—and these not the least important—were inevitably concerned with the position in that system of the law-making and the law-enforcing authorities, with the position, that is, of the legislature and the executive, and, more particularly, with their relationship one to the other. Thus, an initial article declared the French government to be monarchical in character (Art. 1). As a consequence, various articles dealt with the position of the king. The person of the monarch was held to be "inviolable and sacred" in the sense that he was not directly subject to judicial process (Art. 15).[6] The king was recognized to be

---

[6] This matter was much discussed following the failure of the king's flight. Cf. Ch. IX, pp. 201–204.

the fountain of justice (Art. 14) and the fountain of honor (Art. 28). "Supreme executive power" was asserted to reside "exclusively in his hands" (Art. 3). Hence the king was said to possess "the various prerogatives" of an independent executive (Art. 13). Such prerogatives of course included execution of the laws, command of the armed force, power of appointment, and so on (Art. 14; Arts. 17 *et seq*). So far as legislative power was concerned, stipulation was made for the existence of an "Assembly of the Representatives of the Nation." This body, in addition to being possessed of law-making authority, was recognized to have the power of the purse, its consent being declared necessary for the validity of taxation and its control over expenditure, with attendant accountability on the part of "administrators of public funds," being expressly stipulated. On the other hand, joint authority of the king and Assembly was in certain respects determined. Thus, Assembly and king were vested "conjointly" with the exercise of legislative power, the sanction of the monarch being required for laws and the king being declared "an integral part of the legislative body." Likewise, treaty making and other elements in the conduct of foreign relations were recognized as falling within the royal prerogative, but approval by the legislative body was to be necessary. The king was vested with authority to convene special sessions of the legislative body. On the other hand, no mention, it should be underlined, was made of the all-important power of dissolution. Finally, the ministers, though political responsibility of the kind associated with parliamentary government was clearly not envisaged, were not only implicitly but likewise explicitly recognized to form the principal connecting link between king and Assembly. They were to be the king's ministers, but they were to be legally responsible to the Assembly. Article 24 was worded as follows: "The king shall be absolute master of the choice of his ministers and of the members of his council." The article on ministerial responsibility, which from the nature of the case is of the highest interest, was couched in the following terms: "The ministers and other agents of royal authority shall be responsible for all infractions they commit of the laws, whatever may be the orders they shall have received; and they shall be required to be punished for them upon prosecution by the representatives of the nation (Art. 7)."

The Declaration of the Rights of Man and of the Citizen

The National Assembly, in addressing itself to the problem of giving to France a constitution, followed the order of procedure that had been advocated by its Committee on the Constitution. That is to say, the Assembly first formulated a declaration of rights and then undertook the task of drawing up a constitution proper, a body of stipulations, in other words, to regulate the structure and function of government. The first part of the undertaking was accomplished within a month. The second, though it was begun immediately after completion of the first, required two years. In the result, the famous Declaration of the Rights of Man and of the Citizen, adopted in August of 1789, was, as is well known, placed at the head of the Constitution in 1791.

On 29 July 1789, two days after the reading of the reports from the Committee on the Constitution, the National Assembly adopted as its internal law a code of rules of procedure. On the following day, the Assembly, in accordance with the procedure that was thus established, resolved itself into thirty sections (*bureaux*),[7] for the purpose of discussing a declaration of rights. A contemporary account of the dis-

---

[7] Cf. R. Bonnard, *op. cit.*, p. 124.

cussion is not altogether favorable to the procedure employed:

It appears that these particular assemblies do not fulfill the object that was contemplated. In several sections, discussion concerning the declaration of rights ended after very little consideration. In others, all the different drafts that had so far been presented were rejected.[8]

This beginning, like the discussion of Lafayette's motion on 14 July, was in general symptomatic of the debates out of which the Declaration of the Rights of Man and of the Citizen finally emerged. That is to say, the debates proceeded largely without order, unity, or plan. Their course was tortuous, and extended attention to the details would scarcely repay the effort.

In plenary session of the National Assembly, constitutional debate was begun on 1 August. At that time, the Assembly addressed itself to the following question: "Shall there or shall there not be put at the head of the constitution a declaration of the rights of man and of the citizen?" Fifty-six members put down their names to participate in the debate. As was inevitable, only a minor fraction of these took part in the long discussion, concerning which the president of the Assembly observed at the end that it had, even though many speakers were still left, manifestly tired the Assembly. The diffuse and abstract speeches were continued on 3 August, and the debate was brought to an end on 4 August. Contemporary description of the last day is eloquent of the character of the discussion. "This sitting," runs an account, "was very tumultuous. The Assembly was impatient to proceed to a vote. Fatigued by the same discussion for three days, exasperated by repetition, it wished to end a delibera-

[8] *Moniteur*, 1789, no. 29 (29–30 July), p. 124.

tion the matter of which had been so long debated." [9] The Assembly decided almost unanimously that the declaration should be placed at the head of the constitution.

The decision of 4 August concerning the Declaration of Rights, owing to the famous events that followed during that night and to the immediate effects of these happenings, was not followed by further Assembly action for more than a week. On 12 August a motion was made and carried that a committee of five should be appointed to study the various drafts of declarations of rights and present to the Assembly a draft that should form a basis for discussion. The committee, on 17 August, speaking through Mirabeau, made its report. This report and the draft proposed in it were the subject of extended debate on the two following days. After a discussion which demonstrated, as Mirabeau had said, that it is much easier to agree on having a declaration of rights than on what it should be, the National Assembly almost unanimously rejected the committee draft as a basis for discussion.

The National Assembly, having decided to take a poll on all the various draft declarations before it, in order that the draft receiving the greatest number of votes should be considered article by article as a basis for discussion, narrowed the field down to three proposals—those of Lafayette, of Sieyès, and of the Sixth Section. The poll was favorable to the last of these. Hence for the next seven days the draft of the Sixth Section was the subject of discussion. Eventually, however, only a few of the twenty-four articles of this draft were adopted. As a beginning, the Assembly voted to accept the preamble to the draft of the committee of five, the product largely of Mirabeau's pen. Its terms constitute the most interesting and important part of the famous document for which it serves as a preface. In spite of its ornate style, it

[9] *Ibid.*, no. 33 (3–4 Aug.), p. 138.

is an excellent expression of prevailing political philosophy. Then, following adoption of this preamble, the Assembly, by a procedure which consisted for the most part of voting the suppression of several of the articles proposed by the Sixth Section and of formulating in the course of discussion articles in their places, succeeded in adopting one after the other seventeen articles. The seventeenth article was adopted on 26 August, and, on the following day, the Assembly decided to refuse consideration to further articles.

On 2 October the president of the National Assembly informed that body that he had presented to the king the Declaration of the Rights of Man and of the Citizen. The king, the president said, had stated that he would in the near future inform the Assembly of "his intentions in this regard." Three days later, the president read to the Assembly the reply of the king. In a statement that dealt for the most part with other matters, the king at the end asserted that he would not concern himself at length with the Declaration of Rights. "It contains," he said, "some very good maxims well calculated to guide your labors." He then concluded: "But it includes principles susceptible of explanation and even of different interpretation, which can be justly appreciated only at the moment that their true sense is fixed by the statutes for which the declaration will serve as a foundation."

The method by which the justly famous Declaration of the Rights of Man and of the Citizen was formulated and adopted is sufficient explanation of the fact that it is neither a logically arranged nor a symmetrical document. In the matter of the substance of the articles themselves, only approximately half, and those displaying little co-ordination, deal with rights in the usual sense of the word.[10] Of the others, some are concerned with the highly important concept of *equality*, and the remainder enunciate new principles

[10] Cf. Deslandres, *op. cit.*, I, 73 ff.

of public law. It is naturally among these last that are to be found the provisions which are of real relevance to the problem of parliamentary government.

The article of the Declaration of Rights that incorporates the principle of the sovereignty of the nation was adopted by the National Assembly at the end of the first day of discussion. Much time had been consumed by discussion and adoption of a preamble, by reading and debate of the first ten articles of the Sixth Section draft, and by discussion of motions to suppress the first ten articles and adopt others in their place. Finally, at a late hour, when the galleries were empty and the Assembly was so bored as to appear incapable of decision, Mounier aroused the members from their lethargy by suggesting to them three articles. These were adopted. They became the first three articles of the Declaration. The third is worded as follows: "The principle of all sovereignty resides in the nation. No body, no individual can exercise authority that does not expressly emanate from it." Though the author of the article was Mounier, the recognized source of the principle was Locke.[11] Acceptance of the principle was, in the circumstances, a momentous step.

Article 3 of the Declaration of Rights, which asserted the principle of the sovereignty of the nation, posed, as squarely as words can do, the basic problem of parliamentary government. If a sovereign nation is to exist alongside a traditional sovereign, the king, then the matter of their interrelationship becomes a question that must find practical solution. The solution which is afforded by parliamentary government is, of course, ministerial responsibility, a concept with which Article 15 of the Declaration of Rights came to be concerned.

On what proved to be the last day of debate on the articles

[11] Cf. A. Esmein, *Eléments de droit constitutionnel français et comparé* (8th ed.; Paris, 1937), I, 595n.

of the Declaration of the Rights of Man, the National Assembly arrived at discussion of Article XXIII of the draft proposed by the Sixth Section. This article was worded as follows: "Society has the right to demand from every public agent an accounting for his administration." This text was adopted without change as Article 15 of the Declaration of Rights. In the course of such discussion as the article received, no significant views were expressed concerning ministerial responsibility. The reason for the paucity of views with respect to a matter so momentous was in fact simple. The speakers found themselves unable to discuss the concept of responsibility without becoming involved in procedural difficulty. They inevitably tended either to bring in the power of the purse, which had already been dealt with in the previous article, or to anticipate the principle of the separation of powers, which was to be the subject of the succeeding article. In the result, after a discussion that was recognized not to be strictly relevant, the article on ministerial responsibility was unanimously adopted.

The ministerial responsibility that was envisaged in Article 15 of the Declaration of Rights was, in accordance with the general attitude manifested in the *cahiers*, not political but legal. The views that prevailed were, it may be repeated, largely determined by the principle of the separation of powers, a doctrine that was dealt with in Article 16 of the Declaration.

Article XXIV of the draft by the Sixth Section was couched in the following terms: "Every society in which the guarantee of rights is not assured and the separation of powers secured has no constitution." The Assembly made no change in this wording, and the article became, it may be repeated, Article 16 of the Declaration. Discussion of the article was understandably brief, the principle of the separation of powers having already been considered at some length in connection with responsibility. In the course of the short discussion, however, the anomalous position of principles of public law included in a declaration of *rights* did not fail to be several times stressed.

Spontaneous Working of Ministerial Responsibility

Meanwhile, during the first week of August in 1789, an event took place which, together with its attendant circumstances, is closely connected with the problem of parliamentary government. On 4 August, in the course of the voting connected with the decision of the National Assembly to place a declaration of rights at the beginning of the constitution, the president of the Assembly announced to that body the reception of a letter from the king, accompanied by a note to the president instructing him to read the contents to the Assembly. The text of the letter was in part as follows:

I believe, Gentlemen, that I am complying with sentiments of confidence that ought to reign between us, in acquainting you directly with the manner in which I have just filled the vacant places in my ministry.[12] . . . The choices that I make in your very Assembly indicate to you the desire that I have to maintain with it the most constant and most amicable harmony. (Signed) Louis.

The reading of this letter was followed by widespread applause. The communication was even read a second time, being greeted with the same acclaim. Thereupon, the Assembly decided to dispatch to the king an address calculated to convey to him the thanks of the Assembly for the con-

[12] From the Assembly, the Archbishop of Bordeaux, the Archbishop of Vienne, and the Comte de Paulin were chosen for the ministries of Justice, Welfare, and War, respectively. The Maréchal de Beauvau was at the same time made a member of the Council.

fidence that he had just evidenced to the National Assembly. Formulation of the address was entrusted to a committee.

At the famous night sitting of 4 August, just before adjournment in the small hours of the morning, the president read to the Assembly a letter from the new ministers, in which warm greetings and expressions of respect were communicated to the Assembly. The letter concluded with "the sincere protestation of being willing to exercise any public function only as long as we shall succeed in being honored with its [the Assembly's] suffrage."

The text of the address by the National Assembly to the king concerning the new ministers was not ready for several days. In the interval, the Assembly was, on 7 August, engaged in discussing the provisions of the measure proposed to translate into law the decisions of the memorable night of 4 August, when announcement was made to the Assembly of a visit from the ministers, sent by the king. The ministers were received with applause. The occasion of the visit was admitted to be the disturbing point that the ever-serious financial situation had reached. Necker delivered a long speech, in which he reviewed the problem and stressed the necessity for a loan. Necker had been presented to the Assembly by the former reporter of the Committee on the Constitution, the Archbishop of Bordeaux, Keeper of the Seals, some of whose remarks were of considerable significance as indicating the relationship that was developing between king and Assembly. Thus, the archbishop concluded his preliminary remarks as follows:

We, Gentlemen, whom you have so substantially honored by your benevolence, we, ministers of a king who wishes only to be as one with his nation, are responsible to it as to him for our counsels and our administration. We are intimately united by our love for the best of kings, by our reciprocal and mutual confidence, by our zeal for the happiness of France, and by our faithful attachment to your maxims. We come to lay claim to your insights and to your support, with a view to preserving the nation from evils that afflict it or that threaten it.

It was on 12 August that the National Assembly finally voted the address to the king [13] which had been determined upon as a result of the king's letter announcing appointment by him of members of the Assembly to ministerial positions. The draft address was presented to the Assembly by Target. It was, with several verbal alterations, adopted. The National Assembly, on behalf of the nation, expressed its gratitude to the king for his "confidence"; and it assured him that public opinion would be encouraged and inspired by such confidence and by the king's "touching promise of *constant and amicable harmony*." The address concluded:

Your choice, Sire, offers to the nation ministers whom it would itself have presented to you. It is among the trustees of the interests of the public that you choose the trustees of your authority. You wish the National Assembly to be associated with Your Majesty in the re-establishment of public order and general tranquillity. You sacrifice your personal pleasures to the happiness of the people.

In the context of parliamentary government, nothing could be more striking than the relationship which manifested itself in August of 1789 between the National Assembly and the king through his ministers. The conditions that existed at the time rendered the development all the more remarkable. Many indications pointed to the fact that the future Consti-

[13] The National Assembly, having passed on the previous day a group of nineteen articles based on the decisions of the night of 4 August, beginning "L'Assemblée nationale détruit entièrement la régime féodal," decided to make presentation of the address the occasion as well for delivery of the articles on feudal privileges.

tution of France was to establish a basically different relationship. In the first place, legislative-executive relations were to be established and defined by a written and, in that sense, a rigid constitution. Representatives of people who prided themselves on formal and rigid logic were to reject the informal and flexible relationship that characterizes parliamentary government. Representatives who had come to have an evangelical regard for the doctrine of the separation of powers were, out of deference to this principle, to adopt institutional arrangements that they had come to regard as the only ones consistent with this doctrine.[14] They were to arrange, as had been arranged in the Constitution of the United States, that ministers elected to the legislature should be compelled to relinquish their executive position. They were to make members of the legislature ineligible to appointment as ministers, thus pushing separation in this respect even further than the Constitution of the United States had done. And they were to establish a ministerial responsibility that was legal and penal, as distinguished from political. On the other hand, while the National Assembly was engaged in taking the first steps toward the formulation of this future Constitution of France, the representatives of the Nation applauded the king when he dismissed ministers

[14] Professor Prélot makes the interesting observation (*op. cit.*, pt. I, p. 45) that in the eyes of the National Assembly the principle of the separation of powers "offrait le moyen pratique de conserver la monarchie tout en affirmant la souveraineté de la nation." Of this attitude the author, Jacques Godechot, of *Les Institutions de la France sous la Révolution et l'Empire* (Paris, 1951) offers the following judgment: "A travers de multiples hésitations qui marquent la lente évolution de la pensée collective, la constitution de 1791 sera finalement fondée à la fois sur le droit historique et la souveraineté nationale: la difficile conciliation des deux principes entre lesquels on avait hésité allait instituer une des faiblesses principales de la constitution élaborée."

who failed to posses the confidence of the Assembly, and they repeated the applause when the king chose ministers from among the members of the Assembly. In other words, political ministerial responsibility and parliamentary government were enthusiastically accepted in practice by an Assembly that was preparing to make them impossible in principle. Thus, the constitution makers of France were on the point of missing an important lesson which was present before their very eyes. They were to fail to recognize that where political forces are left free to work along natural lines, untrammeled by rigid artificial regulations, an irresponsible head of state and a popular representative body would inevitably tend to evolve a working relationship between them that is the relationship which characterizes the parliamentary system of government.

IV

A Constitution for France: Early Assembly Discussion (August-September, 1789)

THE National Assembly began its discussions of the Constitution, in the narrow sense of the word, on the same day that it voted the last article of the Declaration of the Rights of Man and of the Citizen. Thus, when, on 27 August, Article 17 of the Declaration had been agreed upon, and after debate on proposed additions had been indefinitely postponed, the Assembly "evidenced its impatience to begin the great work of the constitution." [1] After a short exchange of views concerning procedure, the proposal was made that there should be read the eleven articles which had been presented by Clermont-Tonnerre on 27 July as representing the points on which the *cahiers* displayed general agreement. The reading of these articles was followed by a short and unfruitful discussion, interrupted by other matters.

[1] As reported in *Moniteur*, 1789, no. 47 (26–28 Aug.), p. 193.

The Committee on the Constitution and Its Proposals

On the next day, 28 August, Mounier, on behalf of the Committee on the Constitution, suggested a simple plan of discussion. This would involve dealing successively with (1) the principles of monarchical government, (2) the organization of the legislative body, (3) the organization of the executive power, (4) the organization of the military power, and (5) the judiciary. Mounier thereupon read, in accordance with this plan, six draft articles that had to do with monarchical government. These articles were taken, with only slight verbal alterations, from the thirty-five articles that had been presented on 27 July as Chapter II of a draft constitution.

On the present occasion, the six articles that dealt with fundamental aspects of monarchy were, it was said, placed together out of deference to consistent and logical classification. With the first of these articles as the theoretical basis of discussion, the debate which had begun so ineffectively on the day before was continued. The draft article under discussion was this:

The French government is a monarchical government. There is no authority in France superior to the law. The king rules only through it; and when he does not command in the name of the law, he cannot exact obedience.

For two days a somewhat incoherent and wholly inconclusive debate continued. General agreement of course existed that France should remain a monarchy. When, however, an effort was made to state accurately in writing the precise nature of the agreement, the agreement disappeared. One basic difficulty was several times expressed in the following simple terms: "There is no exact definition of monarchical government." Various members attempted to supply the deficiency. Lengthy and elaborate expositions were undertaken with a view to fixing the fundamental nature of monarchy or to drawing careful distinctions between various sorts of monarchy. Some thirty or forty proposals in the form of amendments were offered. Formulas were proliferated. Not the least interesting expression was to be found in a proposal that France should be declared a "royal democracy." But the real difficulty grew out of the attempt to define law and monarchy in their interconnection. In this context, a number of members of the Assembly showed themselves to be too rigid in their thought processes to be able to accept the paradoxes which compromises, themselves indispensable instruments of government, frequently involve. More particularly, these members appeared unwilling to see set down in writing provisions which would require and would assume that behind the words of the provisions there should be accepted distinctions between, and reconciliation of, theory and practice, formal and real authority.

Historically, of course, the source of law in a monarchy is the monarch. But where a king is by tradition said to enact law by and with the advice and consent of representatives of the nation, practical conditions bring it about that the advice and consent become of real moment, the enactment of only theoretical and formal importance; and experience suggests that the situation can more satisfactorily be left to circumstances than it can be precisely defined in legal provisions. However, certain members of the National Assembly apparently desired to define in the Constitution the real, not the theoretical, authority of the king. Hence the first two days of debate on the first draft article were inevitably fruitless. As a member finally pointed out clearly to the Assembly, the discussion was achieving no result because it was anticipating solution of a problem yet to be discussed. This was the problem of what was at the time called the "royal sanction." The question of the nature of monarchy and of the interrelationship between monarch and law involved anticipation of the problem for the reason that the second draft article stipulated: "No act of legislation can be considered law unless it shall have been made by the deputies of the nation and sanctioned by the monarch." Accordingly, the two days of debate on the nature of French monarchy not unnaturally served merely as curtain raisers.

Debate began in earnest when issue was joined on the matter of the king's sanction of laws. Such serious discussion was made possible on 31 August through the presentation of two reports, one by Lally-Tollendal and one by Mounier. The first consisted of a list of some ten statements of governmental principles, a list that had been employed by Lally-Tollendal on 19 August as a summary of a long speech delivered by him in the course of the debate on the Declaration of Rights. The report by Mounier took the form of a series of some thirty-five short paragraphs entitled "The Details of the Organization of the Legislative Power." The two reports displayed no divergence on any point of capital importance. More particularly, they were in agreement in accepting the necessity of royal sanction for laws. On this subject, debate continued for some ten days.

Both Mounier and Lally-Tollendal were, of course, members of the Committee on the Constitution. The committee had in practice found itself to be divided along lines which were beginning to manifest themselves in the National Assembly.[2] The expressions Right and Left had already come

[2] Various writings on the Revolution give helpful analyses of the party situation, e.g., Lavisse, *Histoire de France contemporaine*, vol. I, "La Révolution" by P. Sagnac (Paris, 1920), pp. 84, 113 ff.; Lavisse

into current usage, but the debate on the veto was undoubtedly the primary immediate cause of the basic division. In respect of other terminology, the Patriots, as distinguished from the Aristocrats in a division that was clear enough at the time of the capture of the Bastille, themselves tended to become divided. A wing, not large in numbers, came to be called the Moderates in contradistinction with the body of "advanced" reformers, itself destined to undergo further division. On the Committee on the Constitution, the Moderates, in addition to Mounier and Lally-Tollendal, included the Archbishop of Bordeaux (Champion de Cicé), Clermont-Tonnerre, and Bergasse, lawyer representative of Lyon. The "advanced" minority consisted of Sieyès, the Bishop of Autun (Talleyrand), and Le Chapelier, a Rennes lawyer who had presided over the National Assembly on 4 August. At the time of the opening in the Assembly of the debate on the future governmental system, the membership of the committee had been reduced to seven, owing to appointment of the Archbishop of Bordeaux to the ministry. Thus, the Moderates were left with a bare majority in the committee.

In advocating a system of constitutional monarchy, the Moderates not unnaturally thought and spoke in terms of the Constitution that had been held up for their admiration by their chief authority, Montesquieu. This was, of course, the Constitution of England. As a result, the Moderates were, as has been mentioned, known also as Anglophiles. Leaders such as Mounier and Lally-Tollendal, to mention only two names, furnished no little ground for application of the ap-

---

and Rambaud, *op. cit.*, pp. 108–114; Louis Villat, *La Révolution et l'Empire* (Paris, 1936), I, 61; J. J. Chevallier, *Histoire des institutions politiques en France de 1789 à nos jours: Premier cycle, 1789–1870* (Paris, 1949), pp. 38 ff. The subject is one to which a warning against projecting modern ideas into the past is especially applicable.

pellation. Thus, Lally-Tollendal, in the course of his speech
on 19 August during the debate on the Declaration of Rights,
invoked more than once the constitutional solutions of England. For instance, he referred near the beginning of his
remarks to

the English, the people of the entire world, that is to say, who
understand best the science of government. (I am not afraid to
say so; I felt the need to say so.) And when we are scarcely
born in this science, truly there is too much temerity in our
pretending to give low rank to those whom centuries of
thought and experience have enlightened.

Likewise, Mounier, who in the debate on 16 July concerning
ministerial responsibility had spoken of English government
in a somewhat derogatory manner, displayed during the
opening debate on the constitution his true feelings. He
several times referred succinctly to speakers who "dared"
to criticize England. For example, he said:

It was not a year ago that we spoke with envy of the liberty
of the English, with a feeling of commiseration for the feeble-
ness of the power of their monarch; and now while we are still
struggling in the midst of anarchy, to obtain liberty, before
knowing whether we shall have the good fortune to be free, we
dare to cast a look of contempt on the Constitution of England.

Mounier and Lally-Tollendal each viewed as eminently
desirable adoption of several familiar institutions of English
governmental practice. More particularly, they favored a
bicameral legislature; they advocated power for the king
with constitutional safeguards to dissolve the elective branch
of the legislature; and they conceived that assent of the
Crown should be required for the enactment of laws. The
National Assembly, at the end of several days of debate on

these matters—more especially on the royal sanction of laws
—voted against all three proposals. The Moderates, who,
with a majority on the committee, clearly seemed to represent the average opinion of the Assembly, encountered a
phenomenon of which history has no doubt furnished many
examples. Their proposals were defeated by votes from their
opponents on the Right combined with votes from the more
extreme Left.

Debate on the Veto: Other Constitutional Questions

The central issue in early debate on the Constitution was,
it may be repeated, that of the royal sanction for laws. In
the controversy between the Moderates and "advanced"
Patriots concerning this matter, both sides invoked what they
conceived to be fundamental principles. Both sides were in
agreement that the decisions arrived at should be deducible
from basic principles. Moreover, the two sides agreed as to
what these principles were. They were the two important
principles of public law that had been introduced into the
Declaration of the Rights of Man, namely, the principle of
the sovereignty of the nation and the principle of the separation of powers. And yet the two sides, though basing their
arguments on the same principles, managed without effort
to arrive at opposite conclusions.

The "advanced" Patriots, relying on rigid formal logic
and employing inflexible interpretation, contended that if
the assent of the king should be recognized to be necessary
for the validity of legislative enactments, this absolute veto
would place final legislative power in the hands of the king,
an arrangement which at the same time would violate the
principle that all power emanated from the nation and would
result not in the separation, but in the confusion, of powers.
The Moderates, of course, declined to accept this reasoning.

They argued, in the first place, that the "advanced" Patriots erred in identifying with the nation whatever representative assembly might ultimately be decided upon. They contended that, as a matter of fact, both a representative assembly and the king would alike be agents of the nation, so that to give the king an integral part in the law-making process would be in no wise to violate the principle of national sovereignty. The king, they asserted, had in French history constituted precisely such an integral part of the legislature; and, they added, the *cahiers* were in agreement both that the historical monarchical system should prevail in France and that, in particular, royal sanction for laws should be continued. Moreover, a fundamental question of authority, argued the Moderates, was in a real sense involved. The National Assembly, they said, was characterized, in its constituent capacity, not by authority to create but rather by obligation to recognize, formulate, and establish existing principles.

The initial reply here on the part of the "advanced" Patriots took the form of the assertion that expressions in the *cahiers* concerning the royal sanction were not so specific as to be susceptible of only one interpretation. On the contrary, there existed, they contended, different degrees of sanction; and, according to their argument, it was incumbent on the Assembly to accept only such a conception of royal sanction as would be at the same time consistent with the idea of the king as head of the executive and inconsistent with the concept of the king as an integral part of the legislature. On the other hand, in reply to the argument urged by the "advanced" Patriots to the effect that possession by the king of an absolute veto would involve possession by him of final legislative authority, the Moderates rejoined with the assertion that such arguments displayed lack of comprehension of the practical working of monarchical government. From the point of view of actual practice, a king whose assent was necessary for the validity of law did not, according to the contention of the Moderates, make law. Even though the law might in theory be said to be made by the king-in-parliament or by the king with the advice and consent of the legislature, it would be the legislature which actually made the law.[3] So far as acceptance by the king was concerned, assent tended, it was asserted, to become formal. In this respect, the case of England was cited, where no bill passed by Parliament had failed to receive the approval of the Crown since the time of Queen Anne. If, said the Moderates, the king should withhold approval from a bad law, this was to be commended. The king, they continued, was unlikely to veto a good law; but if, to take the worst case, he should do so, this action, they argued, would result only in delay, which might not in itself be a bad thing; and, in any event, it would not be, in terms of the argument, to make law. Thus, repeated the Moderates, no violation of the principle of the separation of powers was involved. On the contrary, argument in favor of solution of the matter in terms of practice was, they asserted, supported by an important practical corollary of the principle of the separation of powers, namely, the principle of checks and balances.

To this the "advanced" Patriots replied that a suspensive veto would be a sufficient, and an even more consistent, check on the legislature. The nation, they insisted, was not really to be feared. The danger, they repeated, was concentration of too much power in the hands of one person. They reiterated that the absolute veto had this very result. Indeed,

[3] A member of the nobility suggested, in the course of his argument in favor of the royal sanction, that if the king were deprived of the sanction, he would be the only person in France not to consent to the laws that were made.

the absolute veto, according to them, was the very definition of despotism. In connection with their implicit acceptance of a distinction between enacting law and preventing an enactment from becoming law, they insisted that "no one has the right to prevent the nation from making the laws." So far as England was concerned, the explanation for the failure of the king to employ the veto was to be found, the "advanced" Patriots contended, in the fact that, partly owing to the corruption practiced in securing members of the House of Commons favorable to the king and partly owing to the power possessed by the king of overcoming opposition in the Lords by the creation of new peerages, the king had no need to employ the veto.

The Moderates, in their turn, opposed the suspensive veto on what seemed to them sound fundamental ground. To substitute such a veto for the historical sanction would, they strongly insisted, strike at the very dignity of the Crown and the majesty of the king. Supporting the Moderates in this respect, a stalwart of the Right, the Abbé Maury, appealed forcefully to the teaching of experience, adding a warning which was in reality a pregnant prophecy. "Remark with me," he urged, "that all the empires that have undertaken to limit the authority of the king have nearly always lost their liberty." The fact clearly was that the Moderates were not partisans of absolute monarchy. It was rather that, on the basis of English experience, they conceived constitutional monarchy to involve limits that were not defined and imposed by positive law but were evolved by historical processes and formulated in tradition and convention. Thus, Mirabeau summarized his position as follows: "The royal sanction, without written restriction, but completely limited in practice, will be the *palladium* of national liberty and the most precious exercise of the liberty of the people." In this respect, the historical royal sanction was in effect, the Moderates argued, a suspensive veto. Abuse was not normally to be anticipated; but if the king should refuse to accept a good law or if the king and the legislature should disagree as to the worth of a law, the will of the nation [4] was certain ultimately to prevail. The legislature, they pointed out, possessed in the power of the purse an instrument that was always formidable and in practice sure of final success. Power on the part of the king to dissolve the legislature was, they added, an effective and desirable means by which the nation could be consulted and could directly pronounce its will.

Such were the principal arguments advanced by the Moderates and the "advanced" Patriots in the course of a debate marked by the participation of many speakers, by long speeches, and inevitably by much repetition.[5] As has been stressed, the royal sanction was the central issue concerning which the two sides came to grips. At the same time, there was some incidental discussion, especially toward the end of the debate, of the two related proposals made by the committee, namely, bicameralism and dissolution. In the course of the discussion, the "advanced" Patriots clearly showed themselves to be hostile to both. A bicameral legislative structure offended their rigid logic as being inconsistent with the unity of the nation, and, on a more practical plane, the "advanced" Patriots were not unnaturally distrustful of, and opposed to, anything which suggested recognition of the

[4] As may readily be imagined, the *general will* was frequently invoked in the course of the debate, each side making such use of the concept as best consisted with its own argument.

[5] Even so, when the debate was finally brought to a close, many speakers were left who desired to take part in the discussion. They were constrained to satisfy themselves by publication of their speeches.

special position that had been occupied by the privileged orders.[6] Power of dissolution they regarded as a weapon of the king against the legislature, as dangerous concentration, accordingly, of authority in the hands of one man, and as a violation of the principle of the separation of powers.

On 7 September the National Assembly voted to bring to a close discussion of the constitutional questions with which it had been concerning itself since 27 August, the day on which it had concluded its discussion of the Rights of Man. Debate on 8 September consisted largely of unfruitful altercation concerning the procedure to be followed in voting.[7]

The next day was that on which a vote on the structure of the legislature had been anticipated, but feelings ran so high and disorder was so great that no vote could be taken.[8] On 10 September, however, bicameralism was defeated by an overwhelming majority.[9]

The capital matter of the royal sanction came up for vote in the National Assembly on 11 September. The proceedings were again marked by disorder. Near the beginning of the sitting, the situation was complicated by receipt of a letter from Necker in which he stated that the ministers had kept the king acquainted with the activities of the Assembly and

[6] Mirabeau, while favorable to the absolute veto, was opposed to bicameralism for somewhat complex reasons. Cf. Chevallier, *Mirabeau*, pp. 75–76.

[7] On that day, however, the Assembly voted what was known as the "permanence" of the legislature, a matter with respect to which there existed general agreement.

[8] The president of the Assembly, La Luzerne, Bishop of Langres, resigned.

[9] The vote stood 89 for two chambers, 849 for one chamber, 122 not voting. Various sources are given for this by George Gordon Andrews, *The Constitution in the Early French Revolution* (*June to September, 1789*) (New York, 1927), pp. 40–41. Cf. Bibliographical Note, pp. 246–247, below.

that, as a result, a report was enclosed setting out the views of the king. This report, it subsequently transpired, favored a suspensive veto; but the Assembly, after somewhat bitter controversy, decided to refuse permission for the report to be read. In the end, the Assembly took two votes on the question of the royal sanction. By a large majority, the veto was accepted. Then, by a vote of some two to one, the Assembly voted that the veto should be suspensive in character.[10]

Resignation of the Committee on the Constitution

On the following day, the majority members of the Committee on the Constitution, owing to the fact that the Moderates had been defeated on the two capital questions of bicameralism and the royal sanction, resigned from the committee.[11] It was announced that a new committee of eight would be chosen. The names of the members of this committee [12] were announced on 15 September.[13] Meanwhile, on the previous day discussion had begun concerning the period of time involved in the suspensive veto. A week later, that is on 21 September, the intervening period having been marked by the institution of a new Committee on the Constitution, the National Assembly came to its decision about the working of the veto.[14] Veto by the king was to have the

[10] The vote was in the first instance 730 to 143 (76 not voting); then 673 to 325 (11 not voting). Cf. Andrews, *op. cit.*, p. 43.

[11] It is perhaps not too fanciful to see in this resignation an example of the early spontaneous working of the spirit of parliamentary government.

[12] Thouret, Sieyès, Target, Talleyrand, Desmeuniers, Rabaud de Saint-Etienne, Tronchet, Le Chapelier.

[13] On 12 September a two-year term for the legislature was voted. Then, on 14 September, the principle of integral renewal was adopted.

[14] In the same period, several provisions concerning the kingship were discussed and adopted, e.g., heredity and inviolability.

effect of suspending the operation of an act, and, in case of passage of the same act by the next legislature, the king was to have authority again to interpose his veto; but, if the act should be passed by the following legislature, no veto was to be possible.

Defeat by the National Assembly in September of 1789 of the proposals sponsored by the Moderates was an event that presents several interesting aspects. Special students of the period are probably unanimously agreed that at an earlier date the National Assembly would have readily accepted the essentials of the English system of government. Manifestly, therefore, the attitude of the Assembly had undergone change, and the English Constitution had lost favor. There were several reasons for this, but by no means all of them are attributable to French attitudes toward England. The simple fact is that within France a change of sentiment toward monarchy had taken place. More particularly, a belief prevailed that the court was continuing to engage in counter-revolutionary activities. The change in attitude was well illustrated by the position of those persons who had argued that the *cahiers* were not conclusive as to what ought to be decided concerning the Constitution. A newspaper aptly summarized the situation as follows:

At this time agreement no longer exists concerning the *cahiers*. The primary consideration at present is rather the will of a majority of constituents. They would have expressed themselves differently if they had been able to manifest the liberty of which they, even though in slavery, did show the germ. Since the exile of M. Necker, the French have marched with gigantic strides toward liberty. In a week, they have done the work of a century.[15]

[15] The *Assemblée nationale*. See the number for 28 Aug., pp. 164, 165.

All this influenced those persons whose support of monarchy was not strong, and it made more difficult and uncongenial the task of sincere advocates of monarchy. Distrust of the king and his advisers, already widespread, was fanned into flame by the popular leaders. The veto had been seized upon as a pretext.

The National Assembly, from the very beginning of its debate on the royal sanction, had been made officially aware of the aroused feelings that existed on the outside, especially in Paris. On 31 August extracts from letters and other documents were read to the Assembly indicating that an agitated populace was being urged, especially at the Palais-Royal, to move on Versailles, that a resolution had been proposed suggesting the recall of the Parisian members of the Assembly, and that threats were being made against members who supported what was called the *absolute veto*. The Assembly with dignity and courage decided to ignore the situation, but some members were undoubtedly influenced by the disturbed conditions that prevailed. One aspect of the situation was, though indubitably dangerous, not without its amusing side. It was reflected in stories concerning the way in which the ignorance of the people was played upon. For example, some people seem to have thought, according to a speech by de Virieu, that the veto was a kind of tax, one orator being reported to have declared that it was the most cruel tax ever proposed in France. Another speaker is said to have asserted that the blackguard, Veto, ought to be hanged.[16]

[16] All this is reported in *Courrier de Versailles à Paris*, no. 65, 7 Sept. (as given in Andrews, *op. cit.*, p. 32). Madame de Staël wrote: "On parloit du *veto* dans les rues de Paris comme d'une espèce de monstre qui devoit dévorer les petits enfans." See *Considérations sur les principaux événemens de la Révolution françoise, ouvrage posthume de Madame la baronne de Staël*, ed. by the Duc de Broglie and the Baron de Staël (Paris, 1818), I, 319.

One aspect of the distrust that the "advanced" Patriots in the National Assembly felt for royal authority is perhaps worthy of comment at this point. These members seem undoubtedly to have believed sincerely that the whole Constitution, which it was anticipated would be the great work of the Assembly, might fail through refusal on the part of the king to accept it. The Moderates tried hard to establish their contention that there was no question of securing the royal sanction for the Constitution. They argued that the National Assembly possessed full authority to formulate and proclaim the Constitution, and they insisted that the matter of the royal sanction was nothing more than writing into the Constitution a tradition which would apply to enactments by whatever legislature might be set up by that Constitution. Acceptance of a provision for a future constitution could not possibly, they argued, be construed as involving application of the provision to the Constitution itself. The "advanced" Patriots, for their part, feared that a vote to include in the Constitution a traditional principle would recognize the continuity of the tradition and therefore its applicability to all enactments, including not only decrees of the National Assembly in general but in particular the provisions of the Constitution.

In connection with the action of the National Assembly in failing to adopt the English system of government, no little interest attaches to the attitude of the Right. The simple fact, as has been noted, was that the Right joined with the extreme Left in opposing the system advocated by the Moderates. The explanation for this action on the part of the Right was likewise, it would seem, well understood. As Duvergier de Hauranne stated:

All the members of the Constituent Assembly and all the political writers who have left memoirs—Ferrières and Alexandre

Lameth, Mounier and Montlosier, Lafayette and Rivarol—are in
agreement on the fact and on the causes to which it is to be
attributed.[17] The first of these causes was the detestable policy
which led many members of the Right to make the Constitution as bad as possible, in order that it should die more quickly.[18]
This judgment coincides with that of Madame de Staël, who
wrote:

The right side of the Constituent Assembly . . . preferred to
vote . . . in the hope of obtaining good through excess of evil
—a detestable calculation, which nevertheless made converts
because of its apparent depth.[19]

[17] In terms of their particular interest, members of the Right were
undoubtedly influenced in their opposition to the English system by
their attitude toward bicameralism as a French problem. The members of the old aristocracy feared that a second chamber would give
rise to a new aristocracy.

[18] *Loc. cit.*, p. 78. Mirabeau, it may be recalled, subsequently
adopted this *politique du pire*. Cf. Chevallier, *Mirabeau*, pp. 262 ff.

[19] *Op. cit.*, I, 318–319.

V

Ministerial Responsibility
and a Written Constitution

DEFEAT in the National Assembly of the Anglophile proposals, and the consequent resignation of the Committee on the Constitution, may be regarded as bringing to an end a first period in the constitutional history of the Assembly for the year 1789. In this period, the outline of the fundamental structure of the future Constitution of France had been determined. A second short period may be considered to have extended from the end of the first period to the first week in October. During these days, basic articles which filled in, so to say, the outline determined upon in the immediately preceding period were discussed and adopted. Thus, the Assembly, after having on 21 September decided upon the practical working of the suspensive veto, returned on the following day to the specific proposals that had been made by the former Committee on the Constitution. On that day and the succeeding days, various proposals were debated, often amended, and finally adopted. In this way, an executive, a legislature, and a judiciary gradually emerged.

On 29 September the new Committee on the Constitution

presented through the distinguished lawyer, Thouret, a representative of Rouen, a long report. This dealt with such basic matters as the territorial subdivision of the country, the electorate, and local agencies; but the course of discussion in the Assembly was not altered. Finally, on 1 October Mirabeau proposed and the Assembly adopted a suggestion that the articles which had already been voted, nineteen in number, should, together with the seventeen articles of the Declaration of the Rights of Man, be presented to the king for his approval. Accordingly, on the following day the two groups of provisions were sent to the king. Louis at first insisted on qualifying his acceptance, but the Assembly insisted on acceptance "pure and simple"; and on 5 October in the evening, when the famous crowd of women from Paris were already in Versailles and pressing round the royal palace, the king gave in.

On 7 October 1789 the National Assembly returned to its work on the future Constitution of France. At that time, the importance of the turning point in the general course of affairs in France, represented by the critical days of the first week in October, was soon manifest in the Assembly. Members of the body appeared to have for the moment little interest in constitutional matters. In that realm it confined itself to voting some five articles concerned with formalities and formulas in connection with the presentation of legislation to the king and with its promulgation by him. These relatively unimportant articles were discussed, amended, and voted in the course of three days. Thereafter, other questions forced the Constitution temporarily into the background. More particularly, activity in the National Assembly was affected by the fact that a move to Paris was anticipated by the Assembly, where it would be near the king, who indicated his intention of remaining in that city.

The National Assembly held its first meeting in Paris on

19 October. On that day, it voted to proceed with the committee plan on the municipal organization of France. About
the middle of December, a municipal law was voted, and,
a few days later, acts dealing with related subjects were
passed.[1] These decisions had of course been preceded by
discussion, and they followed discussion and decision that
were concerned with other matters. More particularly, the
new territorial division of the country, which has had such
far-reaching effects on French administration, became an
accomplished fact. In other words, from 19 October to the
end of the year 1789, the National Assembly, though it concerned itself fairly continuously with constitutional questions, did not in general deal with questions that were of
immediate interest to the study of parliamentary government.

Mirabeau's First Defeat (September)

In the course of the discussion and votes that took place
in the National Assembly during the last days of September,
one subject was dealt with that was directly relevant to the
problem of parliamentary government. This was the basic
matter of ministerial responsibility. On 29 September the
National Assembly, continuing on the basis of the long
Thouret report its discussion of the proposals of the former
Committee on the Constitution, arrived in due course at the
draft article defining the responsibility of ministers.[2] The
article, as proposed by the committee, was phrased as fol-

[1] Regarded as closely connected with territorial arrangements
were not only local representative assemblies but also local "primary
assemblies," the grouping, that is, of the voters in the several divisions of the country. This, in turn, was considered to necessitate
discussion of the electorate and the method of choosing the national
legislature.

[2] The *Archives parlementaires* also place at this time a report by
Target on the structure of the proposed legislative body.

lows: "Ministers and other agents of authority shall be responsible for all infractions of law that they commit, whatever may be the orders they may have received." This provision clearly implied that ministerial responsibility was to be legal in character. It also undertook to establish the principle that a minister could not plead the command of the king. But it failed to recognize the importance of the power of the purse in connection with responsibility. Accordingly, a member of the new Committee on the Constitution, Desmeuniers, representative of Paris, arose at once to suggest that the responsibility of ministers should be recognized to extend to "their expenditures also." Thereupon, according to somewhat sparse records, a member of the nobility proposed "that this responsibility should have no other effect than to require accounting for expenditures." He added: "If a minister makes a treaty with a neighboring nation, it is not just to attribute to him the results." In the absence of context, the meaning which the nobleman had in mind is not clear. Possibly his suggestion was merely prompted by the reactionary view that accountability of the king's ministers ought to be reduced to a minimum. As a matter of fact, one might have thought that responsibility in the case of a treaty could in reality extend to nothing except "results." Certainly this would be true in terms of real political responsibility.

Few members of the Assembly, unfortunately, had an understanding of or an interest in ministerial responsibility that would be political in nature. Mirabeau was, of course, a notable exception. Consequently, his intervention in the discussion in late September was an event of much moment. He distinguished at once between punishment of a minister and, in a case where there might be "merely a well-known mistake," a determination to the effect that the minister could not remain in office. He went on to raise, in connection with the ministers, the question of rules of eligibility. He regretted that the matter, which had been already raised, seemed to have been forgotten. More especially, he desired to see a decision arrived at "whether a minister may be a member of the National Assembly." He reminded his hearers that several members of the Assembly had already been made ministers. These had thought well to resign from the Assembly, he observed; but there was something, he believed, to be said on the other side. "We experience every day," he continued, "the need for information. To obtain it is quite possible, especially in the matter of finance. As for me, who do not fear ministerial influence so long as it does not operate in the obscurity of the cabinet, as for me, who am persuaded that a minister here will in the future be only a single individual in the midst of his equals—I think that we have need of co-operation from enlightened ministers. Of this I have a real example in a neighboring country." His proposal then was that the Assembly should "decide whether being a minister should result in exclusion from the Assembly and whether all those who are advanced to the ministry while being deputies should have need of re-election in order to enter the Assembly." Mirabeau's speech was applauded, and, had a vote been taken at that time, the Assembly would probably have approved the close relationship between legislature and ministers which is characteristic of parliamentary government. Unfortunately, Mirabeau's proposal was ruled out of order in view of the fact that two motions were before the Assembly. His suggestion did not come before the Assembly again for more than a month, conditions having much changed during the interval.

On the occasion when Mirabeau's motion failed to come to a vote in the National Assembly, discussion was resumed of the committee proposal, as modified by the suggestion of Desmeuniers, concerning ministerial responsibility. A further amendment was moved, requiring that orders of the king should be countersigned by a minister. After some discussion and other proposals, the amendment was approved. As a consequence, the article as finally adopted was worded as follows:

Ministers and other agents of the executive power shall be responsible for the employment of the funds of their department, as well as for all infractions of law that they may commit, whatever may be the orders that they may have received; and no order of the king shall be executed if it is not signed by His Majesty and countersigned by a Secretary of State or by the administrator in charge of the department.[3]

Mirabeau's Second Defeat (November)

To the general proposition that the National Assembly's constitutional debates at the end of 1789, after its removal to Paris, were not concerned with matters relevant to the problem of parliamentary government, there is one exception. Beginning in the first week of November, an interesting and important debate took place on the matter of membership of the king's ministers in the National Assembly. This was not, strictly speaking, a resumption of the discussion which was adjourned on 29 September. On 3 November, Target had proposed discussion of the matter in connection with the future Constitution, but the question was adjourned in favor of debate on the problem of municipal organization. The debate was now inaugurated by Mirabeau. In the course of it, the great orator furnished further evidence of his sound grasp on the fundamental character of parliamentary govern-

[3] The text given in the *Moniteur* is slightly different from that given in the *Archives parlementaires*, but the substance is the same.

ment. He had, in point of fact, become convinced that unless traditionally deep-rooted distrust of ministers could be supplanted by employment of able ministers operating in accordance with the principles of the parliamentary system, the monarchy in France was doomed, and initiation at this time of a debate on the subject was part of a calculated plan.[4] Mirabeau, as early as the beginning of September, had begun to argue in his newspaper,[5] the *Courrier de Provence*, in favor of the parliamentary relationship between ministers and representatives of the nation. His contention was that the governmental process would, as a result of this relationship, acquire such increased smoothness of operation as to contribute very materially to relief of the unsatisfactory conditions which continued to trouble the country. Mirabeau's participation at the end of September in the constitutional discussion of ministerial responsibility had been part of his planned campaign. Adjournment of decision on that occasion, when Mirabeau would almost certainly have been successful, had been followed by developments which had convinced Mirabeau of the pressing need for his solution, if the monarchy was to be saved. On the other hand, these developments rendered his success on the later occasion considerably less certain. He had begun to be the object of suspicion, and the very character of his argument could not but contribute doubt as to his motives. As a matter of fact, Mirabeau was, as is well known, in communication with the court, with which he had established contact through the Comte de Lamarck.[6] Particularly after the first week of October,

[4] The details of the development are authoritatively treated by Chevallier. Cf. *Histoire des institutions*, pp. 60 ff., *Mirabeau*, pp. 103 ff., and "The Failure of Mirabeau's Political Ideas," pp. 88 ff.

[5] Cf. Bibliographical Note, p. 444.

[6] His fifty "Notes for the Court," from 1 June 1790 to 3 February (one dated 16 January was unfinished) 1791, are to be found in

Mirabeau was more than ever convinced that the structure and function of the government needed to be strengthened. He, as well as certain important men [7] with whom he arranged to confer at his sister's home, saw clearly that the existing ministers lacked the qualities which were demanded by the critical conditions that prevailed. According to the account of a member of the "Triumvirate," Alexandre de Lameth,[8] who was one of those called in by Mirabeau, an agreement was reached in terms of which a ministry of particularly competent members of the National Assembly was to be placed in office.[9] Inasmuch as the king had already taken ministers from the Assembly and as no legal provisions stood in the way either of such a choice or even of the continued membership of such ministers in the Assembly, the plan which was agreed upon did not, it is interesting to note, involve any formal action. The arrangements, however, were for some reason not carried out. This failure seems to have been what determined Mirabeau to undertake, with the support of certain members obtained in advance, indirectly to bring the plan before the National Assembly by raising again the question of ministerial responsibility.

On 6 November the National Assembly, in accordance with its order of the day, began a general discussion of the financial condition of the country. There being apparently

---

Correspondance entre le comte de Mirabeau et le comte de LaMarck pendant les années 1789, 1790 et 1791, ed. by M. Ad. de Bacourt (2 vol.; Brussels, 1851).

[7] Including Lafayette and the "Triumvirate." Cf. Chevallier, *Mirabeau*, pp. 94 ff.

[8] See his *Histoire de l'Assemblée constituante* (Paris, 1828–1829), I, 180 ff.

[9] De Lameth (*ibid.*, pp. 185–186) is not certain of the reasons for failure. He suggests as a probable explanation opposition by Necker and by the king. For Chevallier's account, see *Mirabeau*, pp. 96 ff.

no serious question calling for immediate attention, the discussion showed some signs of bogging down, when Mirabeau arose to deliver what turned out to be an exceedingly long speech. He employed the first three-fourths of it to describe with great care and in great detail the prevailing financial situation and its interconnection with existing economic, commercial, and psychological conditions. The picture he painted was an exceedingly dark one. He insisted that unless vigorous steps should be taken at once calamity would result. On the other hand, affairs, Mirabeau contended, could with serious effort be placed on a firm basis; and peace and prosperity could in the end be restored. The most hopeful aspect of the underlying situation was, he asserted, the great confidence which throughout the provinces was felt in the National Assembly. This confidence, however, tended to be undermined by misunderstandings and resultant friction between the ministers and the Assembly. He cited a recent incident. The ministers, having been declared responsible by the National Assembly for failure to publish in the provinces certain decisions of the Assembly and having been summoned to give through the Keeper of the Seals an explanation of the situation, issued a public declaration in which they refused to accept responsibility for the generally disturbed conditions in the country, insisting that they would resign rather than do so. The decision of the National Assembly had been taken on 20 October. On the next day, M. de Cicé appeared and gave a long explanation concerning the matter of publication of decisions of the Assembly. The ministerial declaration was issued on 24 October. The ministers insisted that allegations of conditions of lawlessness in the country, for which they disclaimed responsibility, were too vague to be dealt with through written communications. They suggested that discussion by them of the situation should take place on the floor of the Assembly, or at least that arrangements for conferences should be made. According to Mirabeau, this mistaken interpretation of responsibility for the situation had resulted in making conditions worse. However, Mirabeau suggested that a veil should be drawn over past misunderstandings, and he urged that an effort be made to find "the means to put an end to all those misunderstandings that will not cease to arise as long as ministers of the king shall be absent from the National Assembly." All good citizens, he continued, ardently desired the establishment of firm and effective government, an accomplishment that would remain impossible "if the executive authority and the legislative power, regarding each other as enemies, fear to discuss together the common weal."

Thus it was that Mirabeau employed a financial discussion to raise the question on which he thought the future of French monarchy depended. Some fourth of his argument was devoted to advocating and defending the relationship that existed in England between ministers and legislature. With what was doubtless substantial accuracy, though he either forgot or ignored the well-known provision of the Act of Settlement, 1701, that was repealed before going into operation, he asserted:

Never during the existence of the English Parliament has any step been taken for the purpose of excluding from it the ministers of the king. On the contrary, the nation considers their presence not only as absolutely necessary but as one of its great privileges. It thus exercises over all acts of the executive authority a control more important than every other responsibility. There is no member of the assembly who cannot question them. The minister cannot avoid answering and being spoken to in turn. Every question is official. It has the whole assembly as witness. Evasions or equivocations are at once judged by a large number of men who have the right to demand more exact answers. And if the minister disregards the truth, he cannot fail to see himself attacked in respect of the words he has used in his answers.

Mirabeau attempted to anticipate the objections that would be raised against the presence of ministers in the Assembly. He foresaw that such objections would take essentially one of two forms. Either argument would be made that no need existed for having the ministers in the Assembly, or fear would be expressed that such an arrangement would represent a genuine danger in the form of potential evil influence. Mirabeau answered at length both of these possible objections.

Mirabeau had a clear understanding of the importance of what has come to be recognized as executive leadership. In particular, he realized that the executive branch of government acquires a rich store of information and experience concerning law enforcement and other practical problems of government and that this information and this experience should be available to legislatures as a basis for formulation of legislative policy. According to Mirabeau, a procedure by which individual legislators could address to the executive personally requests for information did not constitute a very efficacious method, nor was a formal demand for information or for the presence of a minister before a legislature a wholly satisfactory arrangement. In the first case, any or no answer could be given; and, in the second, the inevitable result was slowness, delay, indirection, obscure answers, repeated resolutions, and the like. Mirabeau asserted:

All these disadvantages are dissipated by the presence of ministers in the Assembly. When there is question of giving an account both of the collection and of the employment of revenues, can there be any comparison with an examination that is made under one's eyes? If a minister is absent, every question he ought to have put to him will become the occasion for a debate; whereas, in the Assembly, the question is at the very moment addressed to the minister by the member who conceives it. If the minister is embarrassed in his responses, if he is guilty —so many looks are fixed upon him that he cannot escape them; and fear of this redoubtable inquisition prevents malpractices much better than all the precautions with which a minister can be surrounded who has never to make answer in the Assembly.

Mirabeau then concluded this part of his answer with a series of questions:

Where will ministers be able to attack with least success the liberty of the people? Where will they set out with least disadvantage their views on acts of legislation? Where will their prejudices, their errors, their ambition be brought to light with most energy? Where will they contribute most to the stability of decisions? Where will they dedicate themselves with most solemnity to their execution? Is it not in the National Assembly?

Mirabeau had no fear that the presence of ministers in the Assembly would result in undue influence. He insisted that danger of such influence would be difficult to prove.

Influence of the ministers is, when it does not result from their talents and their virtues, attributable to secret intrigues, bribery, and corruption. And if anything can temper the effect of these it is that as members of the assembly the ministers find themselves ceaselessly under the eyes of an opposition that has no interest in sparing them.

He was, continued Mirabeau, genuinely at a loss to know why the presence of ministers was feared. Fear of vengeance on members who might be marked as victims by ministers appeared, he contended, unreal when it was remembered that despotism could employ against courageous men spies more easily than it could ministers. Laws on individual liberty, he felt, were the best protection against ministerial despotism. "No, Gentlemen," he asserted, "we will not give way to frivolous fears, to vain phantoms. We will not have that suspicious timidity which throws itself into traps from the very fear of braving them."

The concluding paragraph of Mirabeau's speech deserves more than passing attention in connection with the problem of parliamentary government in France. This conclusion began as a brief summary of the orator's previous discussion and ended with a new, but undeveloped, argument:

The principal agents of executive authority are necessary to every legislative assembly. They constitute a part of the organs of its intelligence. Statutes which are discussed with them will become smoother; their sanction will be more assured, and their execution more perfect. Presence of ministers will prevent incidents, will give strength to our procedure, will introduce more harmony between the two powers to which the destiny of the empire is confided. Finally, we shall not be asked for those useless committees in which is nearly always compromised the dignity of the representatives of the nation.

Mirabeau's reference to legislative committees in his unexpected concluding sentence is full of interest in a French context.[10] In the first place, his remark furnished the occasion

[10] For further reference to Mirabeau's views on the committees, see Chevallier, *Mirabeau*, p. 259. The general situation, to which there will be occasion to recur, is strikingly summarized by Aulard in Lavisse and Rambaud, *op. cit.*, III, 107: "C'est par ces Comités que l'Assemblée constituante surveilla le pouvoir exécutif et empiéta souvent sur ses fonctions, au point que, malgré le principe de la séparation des pouvoirs, elle participa de fait au governement de la France." It may be recalled that the king, in his declaration at the time of his attempted flight, vigorously attacked the committees. Cf. Villat, *op. cit.*, I, 112.

for one of the principal arguments employed in debate on the
following day in opposition to the proposal of Mirabeau.
Beyond that, his argument seems at the present day a pro-
phetic anticipation of the famous *comités*, more especially
of the Committee of Public Safety, of the Convention and
the Reign of Terror. Finally, this unfavorable reference to
the relationship between legislative committees and ministers
under a parliamentary system is most striking and significant
in connection with the part played by committees under the
Third and Fourth Republics. This has been a role that is of
the utmost importance in connection with the modification
of parliamentary government in France through development of the indigenous characteristics of the French version
of that system.[11]

Mirabeau, at the conclusion of his speech on 6 November,
proposed a measure which fell into three parts. The first two
had to do directly with finance. The third section, which
was concerned with ministerial responsibility, was couched
in the following terms: "That the ministers of His Majesty
shall be invited to come and assume in the Assembly a consultative voice, until the Constitution shall have fixed the
rules which shall be followed with regard to them." In general, subsequent speakers addressed themselves to the whole
of the Mirabeau proposal, but, with few exceptions, the
tendency was for emphasis to be placed on the third part.

Aside from Mirabeau, the members of the National As-

[11] Reference in this respect may be made, for the Third Republic,
to R. K. Gooch, *The French Parliamentary Committee System*
(New York, 1935), especially ch. vii, and, for the Fourth Republic,
to Michel Debré, "Trois caractéristiques du Système parlementaire
français," *Revue française de science politique*, V (Jan.–March,
1955), 28–34. The Constitution of the Fifth Republic, it is not without interest to note, stipulates with respect to standing committees
that "le nombre est limité à six dans chaque assemblée" (Art. 43).

sembly who took part on 6 November in the discussion of ministerial responsibility were favorable in a proportion of more than two to one to the principle of the presence of ministers in the Assembly. For the opposition, the lead was taken by a doctor of medicine of the Left, Blin, representative from Nantes. Not having prepared a full speech, he confined himself to suggesting that in England the presence of the Lord Chancellor in Parliament had always been "more injurious to liberty than useful to public administration" and was to be attributed to the practice of taking ministers from among the members of Parliament. Blin urged that, in view of his lack of preparation and in view of the importance of the subject, the discussion should be adjourned,[12] a proposal in which he was supported by a reactionary noble, Montlosier, representative of Auvergne. The Vicomte de Noailles likewise favored adjournment, contending that English experience was far from encouraging. He insisted that "in England true friends of liberty regard as infinitely dangerous the practice here proposed." He continued: "The minister in Parliament surrounds himself with an army in his pay, he distributes posts, etc. Ministers will exert a like influence among us, an influence extending even to elections." He urged study and reflection, lest French liberty be compromised.

On the other side, however, the forces were stronger. Mirabeau had numerous supporters. Even where amendment was suggested, the principle was accepted. For example, Mirabeau's lawyer friend, Duquesnoy, representative of Bar-

[12] This was the position of Blin on 6 November according to the *Moniteur*. The *Archives parlementaires* suggest that Blin made an extended speech in opposition on this occasion. However, the speech reported is substantially the same as that given by both the *Moniteur* and the *Archives* as made on the following day. It would hardly seem likely that Blin made the same speech twice.

le-Duc, advocated an arrangement similar to one that prevailed in England, namely, the practice whereby ministers
taken from the House of Commons should be required to
seek re-election; and another member, Custine, noble representative of Metz, reflected the important constitutional
principle that ministerial responsibility is in the long run
based on financial control, by arguing that the only minister
who was needed in the Assembly was the Minister of Finance. Other speakers emphasized the arguments made by
Mirabeau. For instance, the liberal Comte de Montmorency,
representative of Montfort-l'Amaury, insisted that the proposal was simple and clear, that it could be easily discussed
without postponement, and that it ought to be voted at once.
He reminded members that "the Assembly would have been
spared precious moments and very long debates if ministers
had been present." Perhaps the strongest support came from
Clermont-Tonnerre. After briefly approving the financial
sections of Mirabeau's proposal, he came to the third part,
which he asserted to involve "one of the foremost means to
prosperity, to grandeur, and to liberty for the nation." He
continued:

We have often groaned under inept ministers; and the despotism
of inept ministers is for free men the most humiliating of all
curses. But a minister admitted among you will in four days no
longer be a minister, or else he will not be inept. I know the
danger of great talents united with bad intentions; but what
would the minister who might possess them do when he finds
himself in the midst of you, who have great talents and pure
intentions? Ministers will at last see men who do not fear them,
whereas now they are condemned to see only flatterers and
secretaries who are occupied in preparing for them means of
oppressing us. The man who has been sold will blush in the

presence of him who has bought his vote. His embarrassment, his uneasiness, everything will betray him. You know how redoubtable are cabinet intrigues. Is a minister the enemy of the nation? He is an invisible enemy when he is not here. If he is admitted, he will be known. In every kind of combat, I know nothing more dangerous than to have to fight over nothing and against no one.

Such evidence as is available suggests that on 6 November opinion in the National Assembly was, particularly after the speech of Mirabeau, favorable to the suggestion that ministers might have seats in the Assembly. However, the parliamentary situation became somewhat confused. The three parts of Mirabeau's proposal did not form an organic whole. More especially, the most interesting section, the third, was manifestly separable from the preceding provisions. Nevertheless, certain modifications having been suggested, adjournment was proposed with respect to all three parts of the measure. Adjournment was voted in connection with the first two articles, after which the question of adjournment of discussion of the third article was put. Two ballots were indecisive. The solution that was then determined upon consisted of postponing until the following day the vote on adjournment.[13]

The impression seemed to be general that Mirabeau's measure would be adopted. As a matter of fact, conditions changed greatly within the course of twenty-four hours. More especially, Mirabeau personally was made the object of suspicion and attack. The Archbishop of Bordeaux, who in an appearance before the Assembly on 21 October had

[13] This was, of course, equivalent to adjournment for twenty-four hours in the sense that the vote on Mirabeau's proposal was not taken on the day the measure was introduced.

spoken of the ministers as "deprived of the precious advantage of communicating with you," [14] felt, not without reason, that adoption of Mirabeau's proposal would render his position as Keeper of the Seals insecure. He sounded the alarm to his friends, telling them that Mirabeau had been in communication with the court. On the other hand, the Right was kept in ignorance of Mirabeau's relations with the court. Hence the forces of reaction continued to view as an enemy the man who considered himself the last hope for the preservation of the monarchy, an attitude in which they were encouraged by Mirabeau's opponents on the Left. As a consequence, Mirabeau on the following day found himself opposed by the same combination of Right and Left that had earlier appeared.[15]

On 7 November the first item on the order of the day was continuation of the discussion concerning the third part of the motion made by Mirabeau on the previous day. The fact that conditions had changed since the day before was at once evident. Montlosier, who on the previous day had confined himself to suggesting adjournment, now led the attack. He declared:

This motion is vicious in principle, dangerous in its consequences, and pernicious in its effects. We cannot in this Assembly give influence to individuals who have received no appeal

[14] On that occasion he had declared: "Messieurs, je viens vous offrir les éclaircissements que vous pouvez désirer, et qui sont rélatifs aux fonctions qui m'ont été confiées par le roi. Devenu dépositaire du sceau de la loi, sans avoir cessé d'être membre de cette assemblée, ma première parole a été de professer hautement la responsabilité des ministres; et je verrai toujours avec satisfaction qu'il me soit permis de faire connaître les principes et les actes de mon administration."

[15] Chevallier discriminatingly discusses the situation, *Mirabeau*, pp. 110 ff.

from the nation. We cannot put in the hands of the government an initiative we have so wisely proscribed.

The next speaker was the noble representative of Rennes, Lanjuinais, a member of the Left who was subsequently to become a strong supporter of the Right. At this time, he displayed the rigid attitude and the strong regard for formalism that characterized the extreme Left. He asserted that his *cahiers* made it impossible for him to take part in discussion in the presence of ministers. The *cahiers*, he insisted, had incorporated into their terms abstract principles for which the Assembly had shown high regard. The proposal under consideration, he contended, violated those principles:

We have wished to separate the powers and what we would do, by giving the ministers a consultative voice, is unite in their hands legislative power and executive power. . . . We would expose them to being the plaything of ambitious men, if there should be found any in this Assembly. Admission of ministers would not produce the benefit that you expect from it. It would be dangerous, it would be useless, every time you might concern yourselves with the Constitution.

Lanjuinais, in his speech on 7 November, alluded to one or two arguments other than those based on the separation of powers. These contentions were fully developed by the next speaker, Blin, leader of the attack on the previous day. He recognized that the proposal, if adopted, would involve only a provisional solution, which would not bind the Assembly when it should draft the Constitution; and yet he argued, no doubt with considerable reason, that the precedent, once established, would be difficult to break. Accordingly he strongly opposed the Mirabeau measure. He undertook to refute *seriatim* the arguments of the author. Mirabeau's support, he suggested, was based on three considerations. The first was the desirability of the information, criticism, and

responsibility that would result from the presence of ministers on the floor of the Assembly. The second was the danger
of committees. The third was the example of England. In
answering the first argument, Blin confined himself to asserting that "ministers can, on the point which is in debate, forward their information to the Assembly, which ought to
reject nothing that tends to instruct it." [16] In connection with
the matter of the danger involved in the employment of committees, the answer was much more extensive than Mirabeau's
contention had been. Blin protested that he could not understand this argument. Of committees he asserted that "the
members who compose them, chosen by the Assembly, are
worthy of its confidence." Concerning such committees, he
continued:

In conferences with ministers, more minute details can be entered into. The kind of circumspection required by a numerous
Assembly can be departed from. The truth thereby gains. And
will it cease to be the truth when it passes into the ears of gentlemen of the committee before it strikes yours? [17]

[16] In the speech (not in the *Moniteur*) which according to the
Archives parlementaires Blin made on the previous day, the answer
on this point is somewhat more extensive, but it is decidedly obscure.
Thus, he is made to assert that ministers are not the only agents who
have information of value to the Assembly, though how he could
deduce from this that ministers ought not to be present in the
Assembly is difficult to see. He suggests that ministers could communicate privately their information to members of the Assembly
and that the information would in that way reach the Assembly.
Again, he asserted that experience showed that the Assembly, on
the occasions when it had summoned ministers before it, had aimed
at embarrassing the executive. In this respect, he cited the recent
appearance of the Keeper of the Seals, a step which, he asserted, had
had Mirabeau's approval. What this proved in Blin's position seems
far from clear.

[17] The arguments in this respect in the speech unreported in the
Moniteur are substantially the same. It is not without interest to

So far as the example of England was concerned, Blin referred to the well-known corruption that was practiced in connection with the House of Commons, and he asserted that the majority which was secured through such practice defeated useful proposals and destroyed the real liberty of the House. "The assembly," he stated, citing the *Letters of Junius* in support of his position, "being reduced to the role of spectator, has no real existence except in changes of ministry." [18] Finally, Blin's peroration consisted of a vigorous, if somewhat dubious account of ministerial responsibility. He concluded:

Through admission of ministers, responsibility becomes a chimera. Having no constituents, they would have no one to whom to answer. Ministers must either direct the Assembly or else give way to the Assembly. In the first case, there is no liberty; in the second there is stultification of the executive power.

Both Lanjuinais and Blin offered at the end of their speeches motions for amendments or additional articles. Thus, Lanjuinais, though asserting that he favored postponement of Mirabeau's motion, stated that, with a view to possible adoption of the proposal and in order to offset its effects, he was introducing an article that he had taken almost entirely from his *cahier*. The article was worded thus:

The representatives of the nation shall not be allowed to receive from the executive power, during the legislature of which they shall be members and during the three years following, any place in the ministry, any favor, any employment, any commis-

---

note, however, that the use of committees is asserted to save valuable time for the ministers. Cf. R. K. Gooch, *op. cit.*, pp. 222–223, and Joseph Barthélemy, *Essai sur le travail parlementaire et le système des commissions* (Paris, 1934), pp. 218–219.

[18] The speech that was not reported in the *Moniteur* is very similar at this point.

sion, advancement, pension, or emolument, on penalty of nullity and of deprivation for five years of the rights of active citizens.

Blin stated that if the Mirabeau proposal should be adopted, he would introduce the following article:

No member of the National Assembly shall from now on be able to enter the ministry during the term of the present session.

Blin's speech was received with applause, followed by demands that the question be put. Lanjuinais's proposal of adjournment was voted down, and, thereupon, Mirabeau's measure was rejected. Next, the additional articles were read with a view to further discussion, and when they had been reduced to approximately the same form, Mirabeau arose to address the Assembly again.

A proposal that the king should be precluded from taking a member of the National Assembly as a minister was clearly aimed at Mirabeau personally. It pushed the principle of the separation of powers to its furthest extreme. Even the Constitution of the United States did not require practice to go so far. Moreover, the National Assembly, a short time before, had been unanimous in approving selection by the king of ministers from its midst and in applauding his assertion that his action had been taken with a view to establishing harmony between the executive and the legislature. The members chosen as ministers had, it is true, seen fit to resign from the Assembly; but Mirabeau had persuasively argued that this scrupulous action was not only unnecessary but even undesirable. Now it was proposed to make members of the Assembly ineligible to the ministry, even on condition of severing connection with the Assembly.

To this proposal Mirabeau addressed himself in one of his most famous speeches. During the greater part of his remarks, he adopted, for a reason that appeared at the end, the rhetorical device of expressing incomprehension and skepticism. "I cannot believe," he began, "that the author of the motion seriously wishes to have the record show that a good minister cannot be found among the elite of the nation." Thereupon, the orator stated a series of propositions which he could not "believe to be the object of the motion," because, as he said, he was never able "to believe in absurd theory." The impossible propositions were to the effect

that confidence accorded by the nation to a citizen ought to be a title of exclusion from the confidence of the monarch; that the king, who in these difficult moments came to ask counsel of the representatives of the great family, cannot take the counsel of such of these representatives as he might wish to choose; that, in declaring that all citizens have an equal aptitude for all employments, without other distinction than that of virtues and talents,[19] there must be excepted from this aptitude and from this equality of rights the twelve hundred deputies, honored by the suffrage of a great people; that the National Assembly and the Ministry ought to be so divided, so opposed one to the other, that all means must be discarded which might establish more of intimacy, more of confidence, more of unity in what may be planned and may be undertaken.

Mirabeau then turned to the subject of England:

Nor can I imagine that one of the means to the welfare of the public among our neighbors can be only a source of evils among us, that we cannot profit from the same advantages that the English Commons derive from the presence of their min-

[19] This is a reference to, and a fairly accurate citation of, the latter part of Article 6 of the Declaration of the Rights of Man. The pertinent provisions are worded as follows: "Tous les citoyens étant égaux à ses yeux [i.e., aux yeux de la Loi] sont également admissible à toutes dignités, places et emplois publics, selon leur capacité, et sans autre distinction que celle de leurs vertus et de leurs talents."

isters, that this presence would be among us only a source of corruption, or a source of defiance, while the Parliament of England is thus permitted to be acquainted at each instant with the designs of the court, to have account rendered by the agents of authority, to oversee them, to instruct them, to make a comparison of means and ends, and to establish uniform progress that passes over all obstacles.

After thus citing the English situation, Mirabeau gave his attention to the existing state of affairs in France and to recent experience with ministers taken from the Assembly:

Nor can I believe there is a desire to do this injury to the Ministry, namely, to think that whoever shall become a member of it ought for that reason alone to be suspect to the National Assembly—or fair to the three ministers already taken from the midst of this Assembly, almost as a result of its votes, that this example should cause the feeling that a similar promotion would be dangerous in the future—or fair to each of the members of this Assembly that if he should be called to the Ministry through having done his duty as a citizen, he would cease to fulfill it for the sole reason that he would be a minister—or, finally, fair to this Assembly itself that it would cause a bad minister to be feared, in whatever rank he might be placed and whatever might be his powers, after the responsibility that you have established.

Mirabeau thereupon put to himself a series of short questions, to each of which he offered a concise answer. If the desire was to establish a principle for the Constitution, the prevailing occasion was not, he asserted, the proper one, nor should so important a question as compatibility of the positions of minister and representative be decided except after careful and deliberate consideration. If the desire was to establish a simple rule of procedure, the *cahiers*, he suggested, should be the guide; and the *cahiers* contemplated no such incompatibility. If the desire was to forbid every representative to offer his resignation, the result, he pointed out, would be a violation of the liberty of members. If the desire was to prevent a member who had resigned from accepting a place in the Ministry, the liberty of the executive power would, he declared, be limited. If the desire was to deprive constituents of the right to re-elect the deputy whom the king might call into his Council, no rule of procedure, he argued, but rather a constitutional principle ought to be established.

Mirabeau then reminded the Assembly of its own actions. "There was a moment," he declared, "at which the National Assembly saw no other hope of safety than in promotion of ministers who, taken in its midst and in some sort designated by it, would adopt its measures and share its principles." Surely, he went on, ministers were not once and for all chosen, without possibility of change, for then a Ministry would be eternal. Moreover, the choice of good ministers was not so easy as to obviate all fear of restricting the number of those among whom choice was to be made, and, no matter how many statesmen a great country like France might have, it was no small matter to exclude twelve hundred citizens who formed the elite of the nation. Surely, he suggested, it was not courtiers or men without the confidence of the nation whom the king ought to prefer rather than the deputies of his people. And then, with manifest reference to Necker, Mirabeau asked: "Would anyone dare to say that that minister in whom the nation had put all its hope, and whose recall it had effected by a most overwhelming and most praiseworthy choice, would not have been able to become a minister if we had had the good fortune to see him seated among us?"

Mirabeau declared that none of the considerations which he had mentioned was a genuine justification or a satisfactory explanation for the measure proposed. Hence there must be, he suggested, "some secret motive." In this way, he recognized that the proposal was aimed at him personally. Having thus placed the argument on a personal plane, he dwelt with withering irony on the rumors and the distrust that prevailed concerning himself. He concluded with a striking proposal:

Here then, Gentlemen, is the amendment I propose to you. It is that the exclusion which is demanded be confined to Monsieur de Mirabeau, deputy of the commons of the Senechausée d'Aix. I shall consider myself highly fortunate if, at the price of my exclusion, I can preserve to this Assembly the hope of seeing several members, worthy of all my confidence and of all my respect, become the intimate counselors of the nation and of the king, whom I shall not cease to regard as indivisible.

Mirabeau's speech, more particularly his concluding remarks, served merely to irritate further the coalition of the Right and the extreme Left. His amendment was summarily rejected.

Only one or two other speakers entered the discussion. One of these, a liberal army noble, De Castellane, representative of Châteauneuf-en-Thymerais, showed no little understanding of parliamentary government. He declared that the greatest advantage to be derived from the establishment in France of a regular legislature would be that thereby "useful men" would become known; [20] "and it would be astonishing," he concluded, "that those who by great talents and

---

[20] This recalls Walter Bagehot's insistence, near the beginning of no. 5, "The House of Commons," in *The English Constitution,* that the "elective" is the "main function" and the "most important function" of the House of Commons, which is likewise referred to as an "electoral chamber" and a "real choosing body."

great virtues might come to deserve confidence would be unable to obtain marks of evidence of it."

The exclusion of members of the Assembly from the Ministry as demanded by Blin was voted 7 November. During the meeting of the National Assembly on 9 November, the president of the Assembly announced to the members that he had received a communication from the Keeper of the Seals in which the king was said to have approved the decision made two days before by the Assembly "forbidding to members of the Assembly entrance into the Ministry."

The fundamental bearing of the formal decision by the National Assembly at the end of 1789 concerning ministerial responsibility would seem to be clear. The Assembly went a long way toward making parliamentary government in France impossible for the time being.

Modern French scholars appear to be agreed that the stipulation preventing ministers from being taken from the Assembly was a misfortune.[21] Thus, for example, Louis Madelin writes: "One of the capital errors of the Assembly was to vote on 7 November 1789 the motion excluding from the ministry its own members. . . . The decree of 7 November 1789—one of the capital articles of the Constitution— sufficed to render the new political order impractical." [22] So also, Marcel Prélot suggests: "The decision which was taken by the Constituent to forbid the choice of ministers in the Assembly was capital in that it rejected the parliamentary system." [23] On the other hand, Madelin expresses the opinion [24] that Mirabeau could not have prevented the Revolution from running its course, though he admits that the great

[21] Funck-Brentano, *op. cit.*, p. 19, is an exception.
[22] In *La Révolution* (7th ed.; Paris, 1920), pp. 106–107.
[23] *Op. cit.*, pt. i, p. 64.
[24] In *Les Hommes de la Révolution* (Paris, 1928), pp. 29–59.

orator understood the situation better than anyone and could have solved it if anyone could have. Similarly, Prélot offers the following striking judgment:

It is possible—but in no wise proved—that if, in 1789, the English example had carried the day against the American model, the monarchy would have been saved. It is much more probable, though, that all the new institutions stood condemned to failure by virtue of a combination of men and circumstances. The Revolution was not yet victorious and neither was the monarchy of the Old Regime definitely vanquished.[25]

In a more general appraisal, Prélot finds that there was "alongside a vast effervescence of ideas a total lack of durable political institutions"; [26] and he quotes with approval Prévost-Paradol as follows: "The French Revolution founded a society; it failed to create a government." [27]

The decision by the National Assembly to exclude its members from the Ministry was, no doubt, inconsistent with its own past action. At the same time, the Assembly once more demonstrated the fact that great difference exists between an informal unplanned development of the principles of the parliamentary system and establishment of them by deliberate written provision. Possibly Mirabeau would have done better to pursue his aims without resort to formal debate and definite proposal. Nevertheless, the fact should not be forgotten that conditions had been rapidly changing and that time had been running against the chances of parliamentary government. The continued existence of a formal Head of State and of an Assembly representative of the nation continued to imply the need for a solution of the problem of their interrelationship, and theoretically this solution might still have been the parliamentary system. On the other hand,

[25] *Loc. cit.*   [26] *Ibid.*, p. 11.   [27] *Ibid.*, p. 15.

the king was much less than formerly regarded as in fact the exalted symbol of the nation. He tended more and more to appear a weak, vacillating, uncertain, and untrustworthy individual. The almost unbelievable distrust that had traditionally been associated with the king's ministers, and more recently with the queen and the king's brothers and the court, tended to be centered in the king personally. Hence literal limitation of the king and of his power seemed the logical solution. The principle of the separation of powers furnished a strikingly appealing doctrinal basis for such a solution. This is not to say that advocates of the principles of parliamentary government had no further opportunity, before the final adoption of the Constitution, to urge their case. There were, in fact, several such occasions. It is merely that in retrospect the parliamentary system seems, so far as the Revolutionary period is concerned, to have received its death blow in November of 1789.

VI

The Assembly and Ministerial
Responsibility: 1790

THE year 1790 was on the whole an uneventful one in the
constitutional history of France. This was true in spite of
the fact that the National Assembly continued with reasonable regularity to deal with various detailed aspects of the
future Constitution.

It should always be recalled that the National Assembly,
unlike the earlier Philadelphia Convention in America but
like later assemblies in France, played a role which involved
not only constituent activities but also an important share
in the day-by-day process of governing the country. As
a result, the representatives of the nation, at the very time
that they were engaged in formulating a written constitution,
were not only acquiring experience in the actual process of
government but were likewise playing a part in, and influ-
encing the development of, the less formal constitutional
history of the country. For, in the last-mentioned respect,
governmental development, according to a well-established
principle of political science, was being determined by various informal extralegal forces as well as by formal legal

provisions. At the same time, these two aspects of constitutional history were, of course, at all times closely related.
More particularly, this was true of such development as
occurred in the direction of parliamentary government.

At the end of 1789 and in the months that followed, the
principal elements of the governmental system—king, Assembly, and ministers—were in regular operation. Natural
unplanned development of interrelations among these elements was possible; and yet the limits, so to say, within
which such development could take place were established
through the legal decisions that had been taken by the Assembly in November of 1789. Not only, as has been seen,
did the position of minister become incompatible with membership in the Assembly, a situation which had presumably
been little influenced through the practice followed by
recent ministers in resigning from the Assembly; but, likewise, a member of the Assembly could not be chosen minister, in spite of the fact that the National Assembly had only
a short time before appeared to sanction, by its expressed
approval, such choice on the part of the king. Within the
somewhat narrow limits thus established, a certain amount
of development was possible. This was particularly true in
respect of the basic matter of finance.

Finance and Control of the Executive

The fundamental dependence of ministerial responsibility
—and consequently of parliamentary government—on the
power of the purse is a commonplace. This situation is of
course, like the parliamentary system itself, the result of long
historical development.

There has prevailed in France as in England the very
ancient principle that new taxation should be imposed only
with the consent of the representatives of those who have to

pay. The corresponding principle of control by these representatives over expenditure grew gradually in close connection with control of revenue. Indeed, where conditions are simple and where need is clear to secure revenue for a relatively specific purpose, no hard and fast line can be drawn between consent to an imposition and consent to the object for which the money is intended to be spent. At all events, the ancient principle that "redress of grievances precedes grant of supply," though it originally meant that consent to raising money should be conditional upon a line of governmental conduct satisfactory to those giving their consent, is at present interpreted, as is well known, to mean that consent to expenditure may be withheld unless government policy is acceptable. In other words, so far as parliamentary government is concerned, the principle is well established that failure on the part of the executive to accept the principles of the parliamentary system can be remedied by the legislature through its recognized authority to refuse to make provision of money for the conduct of government. On the other hand, this authority is of course not normally exercised in actual practice. It has no need to be. The mere existence, without employment, of the authority is sufficient to render control effective.[1] Hence establishment and recognition of the principle, for example by its incorporation into a constitution, are primarily of importance in the realm of theory. Of much greater practical importance in the ordinary course of events are the parliamentary practices that grow up in connection with approval of expenditure. These practices constitute in

[1] Interestingly enough, in the course of the Third Republic, the importance of this basic consideration was particularly apparent not so much in connection with ministerial responsibility, which was too well established to need fundamental reaffirmation, as in connection with the resignation of certain presidents of the Republic— more especially Presidents MacMahon, Grévy, and Millerand.

regular procedure the principal means by which governmental policy is currently examined, debated, criticized, and controlled.

Although the principle of no taxation without representation was, as has been said, considered in France to be an established constitutional principle under the Old Regime, the situation was little more than a theoretical one during the period from 1614 to 1789, when there were no States-General.[2] In 1789 the *cahiers* were practically unanimous in asserting the importance of control by the representatives of the nation over taxation. The practical importance which was attached to the subject was manifested in the declaration of the principle by the National Assembly in June, before existence of the Assembly had been formally recognized. Finally, the Declaration of Rights, it will be recalled, undertook in Article 14 to formulate the principle in the following terms:

All citizens shall have the right, directly or through their representatives, to establish the necessity for taxation, freely to consent to it, to follow employment made of it, and to determine its apportionment, assessment, collection, and duration.

So far as control of expenditure is concerned, the *cahiers* were in general completely silent on the subject. However, some understanding of the importance of such control was

[2] The situation was, it is true, somewhat different in some of the provinces; and there was also some effort on the part of the parlements, in spite of their not being representative in character, to assume the position of the States-General in respect of approval of taxes. Cf. A. Esmein, *Cours élémentaire d'histoire du droit français* (15th ed.; Paris, 1925), pp. 528 ff.; E. Allix, *Traité élémentaire de science des finances et de législation financière* (6th ed.; Paris, 1931), p. 186; G. Jèze, *Cours de science des finances et de législation financière française: Théorie générale du budget* (6th ed.; Paris, 1922), pp. 14 ff.

shown indirectly by insistence in the *cahiers* on the financial accountability of the ministers.[3] This, it may be seen, is reflected slightly in Article 14 of the Declaration of Rights.

In modern times, the lesson has of course been thoroughly learned that legislative control of accounts, being a control after the fact, is, though by no means without value, of considerably less practical importance than previous legislative approval of items of proposed expenditure. The practices connected with this approval naturally vary in detail from place to place. The budget of expenditures being in part a political program and in part a financial reckoning, approval involves not only approval of spending certain sums of money but, even more important, approval of proposed policy; debate on expenditures involves consideration of the two related aspects in varying degree. Whatever the different details of practice are that may be evolved, the general tendency in free countries is clear enough. Representatives of the people inevitably find that the political and financial aspects of expenditure are inextricably interconnected; and debate on proposals for expenditure take, in marked degree, the form of examination and criticism, even if the language is that of finance, of governmental policy.

In the early months of the French Revolution, the curious inquirer could expect to find, if anything, only traces of the beginnings of financial practices that ultimately were gradually established in the orderly working of government. Thus, no budget can be said to have existed at the time.[4] Such

[3] Cf. Ch. III, pp. 65–69.

[4] Lefebvre, *op. cit.*, p. 21, suggests that the report to the king of March 1788 was a budget, which he asserts was the first and last of the Old Regime. In a concise summary of the financial situation at the time of the Revolution, E. Champion, in Lavisse and Rambaud, *op. cit.*, III, 14, writes: "Quant aux dépenses, on n'avait que des renseignements dérisoires."

money as was authorized was appropriated for varying periods and, what is more important and interesting, according to no prepared plan.

All this, however, by no means indicated a lack of interest in financial matters on the part of the National Assembly. After all, finance was, as has been often related, a primary consideration which led to the calling of the States-General; and financial reform was recognized to be, along with formulation of the Constitution, a primary aim and obligation of the Assembly. In point of fact, that body was determined, on the basis of past experience, to lay a new and sound financial foundation by the very act of establishing a Constitution. In this way, repetition of past evils could be avoided. At the same time, the finances of the country were recognized to be in such deplorable condition that the present demanded much careful attention. Thus, with the attention of the Assembly centered on the past and present, nothing could be more natural than that regular control, which ordinarily concerns itself with proposals for the future, should have been little emphasized. The National Assembly, it is true, did not appear wholly unaware of the practical advantages which its control of the purse gave it.[5] Thus, for example, when it was dealing with finance, it showed some disposition to hesitate to approve proposals made to it lest it thereby compromise the certainty of securing the Declaration of the Rights of Man and the Constitution. Necker's popularity assured to his earlier proposals a favorable reception, and yet a tendency undoubtedly displayed itself for the Assembly to feel that it ought to make approval of his suggestions the

[5] Godechot, *op. cit.*, p. 29, quotes the advice given by Condorcet (in his *Réflexions sur les pouvoirs à donner par les provinces à leurs députés aux Etats généraux*) in 1789: "Refuser tout secours pécuniaire, à quelque titre que ce soit, avant que les droits de la nation ne soient reconnus et constatés."

price of securing from the executive some advantage for the nation. Even the modern view of control of expenditure received some recognition. For example, in November of 1789, during discussion of a financial report, a member of the Left, Camus, a representative of Paris, asserted: "It is important to examine all the objects of expenditure in the greatest detail"; and he later added: "By making this examination, we shall throw light on administration." Similarly, in April of 1790, when one of Necker's proposals was, with the approval of the Committee on Finance,[6] brought before a sitting of the Assembly so late as to give rise to a suggestion that the matter go over to the next sitting, the reporter of the committee, the liberal Marquis de Montesquiou, a representative of Paris, invoked in opposition to postponement "the principle of the responsibility of ministers."

Membership of the Executive in the Legislature

In the course of 1790, while the National Assembly was engaged in formulating certain parts of the Constitution[7] and while that body was undertaking to cope with financial difficulties and with various kinds of disorder in the country, a few events took place that are not without importance in connection with the problem of parliamentary government. The first of these events involved a decision on the part of the National Assembly which had the effect of separating still more rigidly the executive and the legislature.

[6] This committee was early established by the National Assembly. It quickly displayed the characteristic of its descendant of the Third and Fourth Republics—the tendency to usurp prerogatives both of the executive and the legislature. Cf. R. K. Gooch, *op. cit.*, ch. vi, and Debré, *loc. cit.*

[7] More especially, those dealing with further territorial division of the country, with the organization of the judiciary, with the civil constitution of the Clergy, and with the constitution of the army.

As early as 26 January 1790, the somewhat unpredictable Goupil de Préfeln, representative of Alençon, called the attention of the National Assembly to the fact that an increasing number of its members had been accepting certain positions that were in the gift of the Crown. The speaker, expressing the opinion that members of the Assembly ought certainly to be above suspicion, introduced a proposal worded as follows:

The National Assembly decrees as a constitutional article that no member, as well of the present National Assembly as of future National Assemblies, shall during the entire time that he is clothed with the title of deputy, accept from the government, either directly himself or indirectly through his children, any benefice, gift, pension, gratuity, charge, place, employment, or other favor, unless by express decision of the National Assembly he shall have been authorized to accept it.

Mirabeau did not enter the debate on this occasion. However, the liberal noble, La Rochefoucauld, a representative of Paris, urged that the proposal deserved careful study and ought to be referred to the Committee on the Constitution. He reminded the Assembly of the English system of re-election of members receiving a position from the Crown:

When the voters have chosen some man to occupy some post, it is to that specific position they choose him. It is right that he should return to them and that he should say to them: "You gave me your confidence when my interests were such and such. They have changed. Are you willing to give it to me again?" It is not the legislative assembly which can judge in that case.

But in the position taken by La Rochefoucauld in this argument, he was alone.

The proposal under discussion, involving as it did rigid application of the doctrine of the separation of powers, struck a responsive chord in many quarters. The remaining speakers who addressed themselves to the merits of the question strongly supported the proposed ineligibility. Their invocation of abstract principle was popular, and their argument based on logical consistency was, it must be confessed, cogent. Since all members of the National Assembly had been made ineligible to be chosen ministers by the king, it was scarcely logical for members to be chosen to other positions by the ministers.

The temper of the Assembly was indicated by the haste with which several members who had already been chosen to positions under the Crown arose and, amid much applause, declared their intention of refusing the positions involved "in order to remain in the midst of the Assembly." Thereupon, similar declarations were rendered necessary by law, for the proposal of Goupil de Préfeln, after modification by several amendments reflecting certain aspects of the debate, was, on the day of its introduction, adopted. The form which the measure finally took was as follows:

The National Assembly, in conformity with the spirit of its decree of 7 November last, declares that no member of the present National Assembly shall accept from the government, during the course of this session, any places or any pensions, salaries, or employments, even after giving his resignation.

In the early months of 1790, one or two other indications were to be observed suggesting that the cause of parliamentary government, if not of necessity finally lost, was scarcely holding its own against views favoring a rigid separation of powers and against legalistic concepts of ministerial responsibility. Thus, in the opening days of February, repeated disorders in the country gave rise to the idea that the National Assembly should, through a proclamation addressed to the people, attempt to exert a quieting influence. Such a proclamation was in fact drafted by Talleyrand, who in September of 1789 had been continued a member of the Committee on the Constitution after the withdrawal of the Anglophile members. Talleyrand's draft, entitled *An Address by the National Assembly to the French People*, was read on two separate occasions to the Assembly. Some slight tendency toward adverse criticism manifested itself, this being based partly on omissions in the address and partly on the doctrinaire character of its language and manner. However, the draft was adopted almost unanimously without change. The French people were assured that the National Assembly had, in spite of serious difficulties, done great things for them. More particularly, the principles of the Constitution, it was asserted, had been outlined, and this, it was proclaimed, would guarantee liberty forever. In respect of the matter which was directly connected with the problem of parliamentary government, this assertion was made: "You have been disturbed by the power of the ministers; we have imposed upon them the reassuring law of responsibility." And later in the address, where criticisms and rumors were being answered, this passage occurred:

We have destroyed the executive power? No: say rather ministerial power. It was that which destroyed, that which often degraded, the executive power. As for the executive power, we have clarified it by showing it its true rights. More especially, we have ennobled it by causing it to go back to the true source of its power, the power of the people. It is now without force? As against the Constitution and the law, that is true: but, in conformity with them, it will be more powerful than it ever was.

Again, at the end of March, Target, on behalf of the Committee on the Constitution, made a short report, which had been ordered by the National Assembly, concerning the progress that had been realized up to that time. The report, after brief statements with respect to the difficulties which the Assembly had been obliged to overcome and with respect to the far-reaching accomplishment of destroying the feudal system, asserted that the bases of the Constitution had been laid. The first particular was this: "You have guaranteed the nation against despotism by means of your law establishing severe responsibility."

Debate on the Power of War and Peace

In May the National Assembly engaged in a debate on a question which, according to the historian of parliamentary government in France, was, in the context of the form given to the discussion, "quite simply insoluble." [8] This question was that of whether authority to decide on war and peace should belong to the king or to the assembly. Most of the speeches, which were highly abstract and largely uninteresting, favored the one extreme or the other.[9] Only a few, such as those of Clermont-Tonnerre and Mirabeau, recognized that the question was in reality a problem of the relationship between the executive and the legislature, the solution of which ought to be worked out by experience through development of ministerial responsibility. However, this solution, necessarily involving compromise and a reconciliation of rigid principles, clearly had little appeal for either the sup-

[8] Duvergier de Hauranne, *op. cit.*, I, 150: "Tant que les deux partis s'accordaient à vouloir que les pouvoirs vécussent d'une vie séparée, au lieu de vivre d'une vie commune, leurs arguments, également vrais, également faux, pouvaient se poursuivre à l'infini, sur deux lignes parallèles, sans jamais se rencontrer."

[9] For an entertaining account of the debate, see J. J. Chevallier, *Barnave: ou Les deux faces de la Révolution* (Paris, 1936), ch. xiii, pp. 134 ff., and his *Mirabeau*, pp. 137 ff.

porters of the king or the champions of the Assembly, both of whom saw in such a solution a violation of formal logic. Nevertheless, it was a compromise that proved, in the circumstances, to be the only practical solution; and an arrangement was adopted almost unanimously which pleased no one, which left behind it controversy as to which side had in reality got the better of the debate, and which scarcely advanced the cause of parliamentary government.[10] Duvergier de Hauranne asserts that understanding of the cabinet system would have easily solved the whole question.[11]

The Disorders at Brest

On 19 and 20 October, a further debate took place in the National Assembly that was in no small degree pertinent to the problem of parliamentary government. In the course of the debate, the question of ministerial responsibility was raised in a form substantially the same as that in which the matter had been discussed, slightly more than a year before, on the occasion of the dismissal of Necker. On the present occasion, however, the discussion was, it need scarcely be remarked, much influenced by developments that had taken place in the interval and by the new conditions that existed.

The debate grew out of certain disorders which had occurred during previous weeks at Brest. These disorders moreover were only one example of a series of incidents that had been taking place for some time. Such incidents were in practice regularly brought to the attention of the Assembly, and announcement of them usually gave rise to some sort of

[10] War was to be declared by the Assembly, but only on proposal by the king; and the decree of the Assembly would need the assent of the king.

[11] *Op. cit.*, I, 156: "Si l'Assemblée eût compris, comme Mirabeau, le rôle des ministres, la plupart des difficultés se seraient soudainement évanouies.

discussion. The discussion was, in the case of the Brest incident as in general, conditioned by the existing relationship
between the Assembly and the king and his ministers. The
situation was, broadly speaking, the same as that under a
governmental system, such for example as that of the United
States, in which the executive and the legislature are related in a manner conceived to be determined by the principle of the separation of powers. Thus, in France during
the earlier months of 1790, the executive was of course recognized to be primarily responsible for the maintenance of
law and order. Where effective steps were on occasion taken,
the executive was commended for its successful handling of
the affair. In other instances, criticism was directed at the
executive, and suggestions were made that the executive
should follow a certain line of conduct. In either event, the
Assembly constantly asked for information and demanded
explanations. Its committees insisted on playing a prominent
part. The executive, in turn, not only commonly complied
with these requests, it also furnished information and explanations without waiting to be asked for them. This was particularly true where the executive felt that some action was
desirable on the part of the Assembly. In other words, executive recommendations were made to the legislature.

All this, it will readily be seen, is familiar procedure in the
relations between executive and legislature that are not based
on the parliamentary principle. Even under parliamentary
government as it has been practiced, the situation, it may be
noted, is not greatly dissimilar in the matter of foreign affairs,
in respect of which, as is well known, democratic control
has been relatively tardy in asserting itself. Thus, in the summer of 1790, the problem of Anglo-Spanish relations as they
affected France gave rise to executive and legislative activities
an account of which would doubtless be familiar in any

democratic country, whether its government is parliamentary or nonparliamentary in character.

The principal variation of nonparliamentary government from the parliamentary system is not that control is nonexistent. It is not that information is inaccessible and criticism impracticable. It is not that responsibility is absent. On the contrary, all these things are, it may be suggested, to be found in democratic government of the nonparliamentary type as well as in parliamentary government. The characteristic distinction is that under the parliamentary system the responsibility is organized, rather than merely potential and moral; confidence and harmony are the basic considerations; and the hypothesis of sanction in the form of anticipated resignation is clearly understood. The existence of monarchy, of course, makes a difference; and yet the English government, say, under William III, was not greatly different in essentials from the traditional government of the United States. On the other hand, under politically democratic monarchy that is not too much trammeled by rigid constitutional provisions, the tendency is inevitably in the direction of the parliamentary system. This is what gives principal significance to the debate in the French National Assembly in October in 1790.

On 19 October a Jacobin patriot noble, Menou, representative of Touraine, made a striking report on behalf of four committees (Diplomatic, Colonial, Military, and Naval), to which had been referred numerous letters and other documents concerning the disorders at Brest. This somewhat lengthy report, after a full treatment of the various aspects of the troubles, proceeded to examine the connection between the particular incidents and the general political situation of the country. The reporter did not hesitate to place the blame squarely on the ministers. "We saw," he wrote, "the regeneration of the state advancing rapidly towards its goal; we saw that it no longer had need of anything except the active and real co-operation of the agents of the executive power; and yet this co-operation is not such as we should have expected." He spoke of "their inertia" and of "the lack of confidence that they have inspired in the people." He complained of their "slowness" and of their "delays," adding that "the public force has slowed down in their hands." The recent almost daily communications to the Assembly from the ministers, announcing disorders and defiance of steps taken by the executive, were, asserted the report, clear evidence that the ministers lacked the necessary energy and force. "Your committees have not forgotten," continued the report, "that it belongs only to the king to name the ministers; but they know that you have the duty of causing the truth to be known, that this is the most sacred perhaps of the functions that have been confided to you. They believe that you would compromise the safety of the state if you should fear to tell the truth to a king worthy of hearing it." The report then concluded:

A decree excludes from the Ministry the members of this Assembly. It ought to be maintained. It is the *palladium* of liberty. The personal sentiments of the king do not permit it to be doubted that if he determines to choose new ministers, he will take them from among the friends of the Constitution. The new organization will be quickly effected and the public force will assume again all its energy, if an intelligent and zealous co-operation prevails between the Assembly and the executive power and its agents.

On the basis of the Menou report, the committees that were concerned offered for the Assembly's approval a long and detailed set of provisions. Following a series of specific stipulations, the conclusion of the proposal was worded as follows:

The National Assembly, after voting the preceding stipulations, directs its attention to the present situation of the state; and recognizing that lack of confidence on the part of the people toward the ministers occasions lack of force on the part of the government, decrees that its president shall proceed to the king to represent to His Majesty that the lack of confidence that the people have conceived toward the present ministers constitutes the greatest obstacle to the re-establishment of public order, to the execution of the laws, and to the completion of the Constitution.

The National Assembly devoted two sittings to discussion of that part of the Menou report which related to the ministers. In point of fact, the interest of members of the Assembly was primarily centered in this aspect of the question. Indeed, at the beginning of the second day of discussion, after some altercation concerning the limits of the debate, the National Assembly voted, on the proposal of Alexandre de Lameth, that, of the three parts into which the question fell, it would "begin with that which is relative to the ministers."

The ministers of the king, it must be agreed, were at this time in an exceedingly unfortunate position. The power of the king had been persistently and consistently confined by the National Assembly within ever-contracting limits. And yet the ministers were severely criticized for their inertia and lack of force. The indictments contained in the Menou report represented, it would seem, the general opinion of the public. In any event, attacks on the ministers were made throughout the debate, and no speaker came to their defense.

For some time past, as has been pointed out, nearly every successful outbreak of disorder in some part or other of the country had been the occasion for finding fault with the ministers and for putting the blame upon them. More particularly, some six weeks before the debate that was occasioned by the Brest disorders, the *Moniteur* [12] noted briefly an event which suggested the trend of dominant sentiment. Near the opening of a sitting of the Assembly, its president was speaking in formal reply to some delegation that had appeared before the Assembly, when "certain clamors" were heard in the Tuileries. According to the account, the noise increased, and soon a large number of voices were to be heard. "In the midst of tumultuous cries," states the *Moniteur*, "these words were a thousand times repeated: 'Dismissal of the ministers.' " This demonstration had undoubtedly been arranged by the more vigorous elements of the Left. During the debate on the Brest incidents, intimation was made by one speaker,[13] without reply, that the populace was demanding to be rid of Lafayette as well. However that may have been, the position of the Left was somewhat complex and inconsistent. The Left was not unnaturally inclined to insist on some leniency with respect to disorders originating with the masses, while vigorously criticizing any failure rigidly to enforce the law against resistance by the privileged classes. Inasmuch as most of the disorders in 1790 were

[12] For 1790, no. 247 (4 Sept.), p. 1020.

[13] The Abbé Jaquemard. He spoke of "les cris que vous avez entendus, il y a quelques semaines, les cris de ce Peuple qui demandait la tête des Ministres, & celle de son vertueux Général." In the same debate a short while before, Clermont-Tonnerre, who neither defended the ministers nor believed that a very deep-running opinion was opposed to them, said: "Il y a six semaines, autour de votre enceinte, 50 voix ont tumultueusement demandé le renvoi des Ministres; aujourd'hui quatre Comités composés en tout de vingt-cinq Membres, ont résolu à une majorité de quinze contre dix, de vous proposer de confirmer ce voeu; & voilà ce qu'on appelle le voeu de la Nation."

counterrevolutionary in character, the Left at this time stressed primarily its advocacy of law and order. It charged that the ministers were shirking their duties not only in respect of maintaining order but also in matters that were involved in the economic rehabilitation of the country. According to a famous epigram of Charles de Lameth, "fourth" member of the "Triumvirate," "the executive power was shamming dead." [14] The motive attributed to the ministers was that of increasing the difficulty of the problems of the Assembly with a view to bringing that body into disrepute with the people. This, according to the Left, placed the committees in a very disadvantageous position.[15]

The basic argument of the Left on the occasion of the Brest incident raised, it would seem, a fundamental question of cause and effect, namely, the question whether the committees assumed power because the ministers were weak or the ministers were weak because of the power assumed by the committees. The true answer doubtless is that both causes were at work, in other words, that reciprocal cause and effect were involved; but the Left inevitably held that weakness of the ministers was the original cause. The Right, of course, refused to accept such an interpretation. In point of fact, divided responsibility did exist, and modern experience shows that executive strength does not flourish in such conditions.

On 10 October, a few days, that is, before the debate on the Menou report, an interesting manifestation was to be observed in the National Assembly of the divergent views of the Left and Right in the matter of committees and minis-

---

[14] *Moniteur*, 1790, no. 295 (22 Oct.), p. 1223; De Lameth, *op. cit.*, I, 185–186.
[15] De Lameth, *op. cit.*, II, 52–53. For a detailed discussion of the situation, cf. Chevallier, *Mirabeau*, pp. 258 ff.

terial responsibility. A communication from a minister was being read by a secretary when a member of the Left, applauded by the Left and not disapproved by the Right, interrupted to insist that, though he would not oppose the reading in the present instance, he regarded as dangerous practice the reading without previous referral to a committee of communications from the ministers. One member of the Right exclaimed: "The committees are not our guardians!" Another saw in the interruption evidence of "jealousy of the members of the Assembly toward the ministers of the king." Similarly, during the debate on the Menou report, Barnave, the most articulate of the orators of the Left, was vigorously criticizing the ministers, asserting that "the Military Committee saw that the most powerful cause of insubordination is lack of confidence in the Ministry and its agents," when the most eloquent speaker of the Right, Cazalès, interrupted with this interjection: "The sole means of re-establishing the strength of the executive authority is to suppress all the administrative committees of the Assembly and to make the ministers responsible."

The Right not unnaturally saw in the Menou proposals a further attack on the position of the Crown, and, in its desire to defend and even to strengthen the royal authority, it opposed the suggestions of a vote of no confidence. Although sharing the adverse opinion concerning the ministers, it took the reactionary position which it had upheld in July of 1789, the position that choice of the ministers was the exclusive prerogative of the king. This was the position that was urged by Cazalès. "If," he argued, "the Assembly by its influence should exclude from the Council men called upon because of the confidence of the monarch, it would soon come to the point of choosing them itself; and we should fall into the most monstrous tyranny." Cazalès had the temerity to invoke "the constant practice of England, of that people which were the first to know the art of liberty." Confining himself wholly to examples from the seventeenth century, he asserted, amid marks of disapprobation: "You will not see in history a single example of a minister dismissed at the will of Parliament."

The Left, on the other hand, firmly supported the Menou proposal and its advocacy of a declaration to the king that the ministers had not the confidence of the Assembly and the country. Thus, Barnave, addressing himself to this question, said:

If the lack of confidence which the nation has conceived for the present ministers opposes the most powerful obstacles to the establishment of public order and of the Constitution, have we the right and the duty of putting this truth before the eyes of the king? Our right is incontestable. Being organs of the nation, first counselors of the king, we ought to make known to the monarch what is necessary for the happiness of the people. Administrative bodies have always enjoyed this right, have been obliged to conform themselves to this duty. You yourselves last year declared to the king that the ministers had not, would not obtain, the confidence of the nation. Then, they acted openly against you. Today, it is a question only of their incapacity, of a voluntary or involuntary inertia. The circumstance is different; the principle is still the same.

Barnave, it may readily be agreed, was on sound ground in insisting on the right and obligation of the representatives of the people under political democracy to criticize the executive. His inconsistency lay, it may be suggested, in the fact that the Left, by being committed to a rigid separation of powers and to a merely legal kind of responsibility, was doing everything to make parliamentary government impossible, whereas he was advocating an expedient, namely, a declaration of lack of confidence in the ministers, which was intimately associated with the political variety of responsibility and with the parliamentary system. The system advocated by the Left called for legal, as distinguished from political, procedure, that is to say, for impeachment. This was clearly brought out by speakers of the Right and Center. They, of course, did not advocate the system of the Left. They merely pointed out what the Left, if consistent, ought to advocate. They urged the Left to propose impeachment, while themselves recognizing the inadequacy of the practice as a basis for effective responsibility. Thus, an uncertainly mild Leftist member who had not previously been conspicuous in the Assembly, Brevet, lawyer representative of Anjou, in a much applauded speech, which was by a large majority voted the honor of being printed at public cost, put the matter in a pointed question: "Who does not see that the conduct of a minister can be very reprehensible, and yet not give grounds for a national accusation?" Barnave himself in the circumstances did not hesitate to take the same position:

If the ministers, in bringing about serious and real evils, have not committed crimes, if, having committed crimes, the offenses are concealed or the proofs have been destroyed, or even if the proofs are authentic and certain—time is necessary for a reasoned accusation to cause them to quit the post in which they compromise the safety of the state.

Barnave was thus recognizing, strangely enough, reasons for considering political responsibility superior to legal responsibility. He even continued: "It would be necessary—for such is the consequence of this reasoning—to allow the commonwealth to perish rather than to formulate against them a general expression of lack of confidence." Moreover,

Barnave, with little consistency but with more accuracy than Cazalès, invoked English practice. With respect to a vote of no confidence he asserted: "This usage is constant with a people who for a long time have known how to govern themselves." With reference to Cazalès he said: "History has on this subject been indeed altered." He continued:

Every time that the proposal which is made to you has been advanced or accepted in England, it has been so as a constitutional step; and no one has regarded it as an attack on the royal authority or on the Constitution. It has rarely been employed, because the ministers, taking part in the deliberations of the House of Commons, can serve usefully only when they have a majority. When they no longer have it, the king, warned that he can no longer retain his confidence in them, withdraws it from them.

In view of the strong opposition on the part of the Left to membership of ministers in the Assembly, Barnave might be thought to be on somewhat dangerous ground. However, he apparently felt no misgivings. Far from seeing in the vote of no confidence a phenomenon peculiarly interrelated with the English system, he asserted with somewhat doubtful logic that it was even more consistent with the French system:

As to the declaration that ministers have lost public confidence, it is certain that you ought to adopt this form even more than in England, where the king is warned by an exterior sign. You have no other means of acquainting him with a truth which in the interest of the Constitution is necessary and which is decisive for him.

He persistently continued, however, in spite of everything to employ the Left's rigid application of the principle of the separation of powers. Thus, he exhorted the Assembly at the end of his speech in favor of the Menou proposal:

Declare at the same time that you persist in the decree by which you excluded all your members from the Ministry. This decree is unshakable. Everyone knows at the bottom of his heart that we shall never go back on it.

Barnave seemed to leave no doubt as to the unalterable opposition on the part of the Left to a close interrelationship between ministers and Assembly. On the other hand, the vigor with which the star speaker of the Left reaffirmed at the end of the debate the principle of exclusion of ministers from the Assembly was possibly due in some part to current partisan considerations. The Left undoubtedly had in view a remark made by Cazalès at the opening of the debate on the day before. At that time, the eloquent orator of the Right had hinted that, just as in July of 1789 the Left had supported appointment of ministers from the Assembly on the ground that public opinion supported such action, so it might approve repeal of the decree of exclusion with a view to entry by members of the Left into the Ministry. Such repeal, Cazalès none the less suggested, would be a good thing.

Although the Right out of hostility to Mirabeau had in the previous November supported the decree excluding members of the Assembly from the Ministry, it now apparently realized that its present argument in favor of the king's unlimited power of appointment was wholly inconsistent with such exclusion. However, Cazalès had reference rather to the alleged intrigues of the Left when he said: "Perhaps if this question should be discussed, the most zealous partisans of this decree would be the most active to demand its modification." He was immediately interrupted by Charles de Lameth, who exclaimed: "Let an amendment be put that the decree shall be maintained." Barnave merely reiterated this point of view at the end of the debate.

No reason exists to question the sincerity of the Left in the matter of its attitude toward the principle of the separation

of powers. There can be no doubt that parliamentary government in its classic form, involving as it does a nice balance
of executive and legislative power, has never received the en-
thusiastic support of the French Left. Its traditional position
has been support of a system in which paramount authority
rests in an assembly, with the executive definitely subordinate
to it. During the debate of October of 1790, this position was
manifest; and it was given the apparent support of abstract
principle by a special application of the doctrine of the
separation of powers. The simple argument in this respect
was of course that the king, if allowed to appoint members
of the Assembly to positions under the Crown, could destroy
the independence of the Assembly in a way that would be
flagrantly contrary to the principle of the separation of
powers. On the other hand, the Right, by a different
emphasis, suggested a different application of the same principle. The object was, of course, defense of the royal power,
which the Right contended, not without reason, was gradually being stripped of all authority. The position of the Right
was ably put by Cazalès at the opening of the debate:

There are in a state two kinds of powers—the legislative power
and the executive power. It is on their entire independence that
public liberty rests. If the legislative body should usurp the
power of appointing ministers (*murmurs arise*), the executive
force would be invaded, the two powers would be fused, and
we should groan under the most intolerable despotism.

There can be no doubt that Cazalès, in thus pushing his
defense of monarchy to the point of completely excluding
legislative influence in connection with the choice of ministers, was on poor ground in terms of the development
which in England was bringing parliamentary government to
its classic form. However, he soon assumed a position which
was in this context much more sound. He raised the question

of the power of dissolution, a matter concerning which the constitutional discussions had been little concerned. Cazalès argued that it was through the power of dissolution that popular influence had its proper play. In this respect, he did not hesitate to come down to the eighteenth century in citing English experience. He invoked the case which Mirabeau in July of 1789 had so correctly interpreted:

Charles Fox was minister. He proposed the celebrated bill that was rejected at two o'clock. At midnight, Fox was no longer minister. He inflamed the Commons, who complained of the new minister, Pitt, who governed and still governs England with so much glory. The Commons alleged that he was unconstitutionally appointed. . . . The king answered that his will was the legal title of appointment. The Commons made a new address; and they declared to be a traitor whoever should advise the dissolution of Parliament. The king answered: "A great question has arisen between Parliament and me; I appeal to my people." He spoke, and Parliament was dissolved.

Cazalès continued:

Such is the admirable constitution of the English people. Such is the happy effect for public liberty of the prerogative of dissolving Parliament, that without disorder, without faction, the king maintains a legal influence over the representatives of the people. Every time that the three parts are in unison, the people obey. Every time that one of the parts differs in opinion, the people judge.

The Left had nothing to say on the question of dissolution. Barnave made no reply to Cazalès in this respect. However, Dupont de Nemours, on the second day of the debate in the Assembly, is reported to have discussed at length before the Jacobin Club the question of ministerial responsibility.[16] His

---

[16] Cf. *Arch. parl.*, XIX, 737–740. There is no mention in F.-A. Aulard *La Société des Jacobins* (Paris, 1889–1897) of the event.

position, according to the report, was the familiar one which envisaged responsibility as legal and which conceived control as effected through impeachment. At the same time, he realized that things in England were developing along a different line, and he held that the institution of dissolution marked the characteristic difference between English and French government.

Mirabeau took no part in the two-day debate on the Menou proposal. Duvergier de Hauranne has suggested that the reason may be found in the fact that Mirabeau's independence had been compromised through the relations he had established with the king and the court:

Certainly it was not that Mirabeau had deserted the cause of the Revolution, the cause of liberty, or the cause of constitutional monarchy, of which he was more than ever the intelligent and devoted servant. But it was no longer gratuitously that he served it; and this new circumstance, without cramping the freedom of his opinions, often cramped that of his speech. In a question in which the royal prerogative appeared to be involved, he did not dare therefore to declare himself publicly in favor of the parliamentary prerogative.[17]

The records, however, suggest that Mirabeau attempted to enter the debate on the first day in order to reply to Cazalès. When the latter had concluded his speech, Ricard, a member of the Left from Toulon, appeared at the tribune with documents in hand. Thereupon, Mirabeau politely pointed out that, in a debate of the nature of that in progress, speakers for and against ought to alternate, that a written speech was not suitable as an answer to the arguments of Cazalès, and that he himself would like to speak in order "to refute his numerous slips." Mirabeau continued by saying that he had

[17] *Op. cit.*, I, 100. Chevallier, in his *Mirabeau*, pp. 201 ff., gives a long discussion of the matter.

no objection to written speeches, of which he himself often made use; but he desired to answer Cazalès, who "from the first word to the last" seemed to him to be beside the point. The Right must have anticipated that Mirabeau would not support the monarchical cause to their satisfaction, for no sooner had Mirabeau made his suggestion than not only Cazalès but another principal debater from the Right, the Abbé Maury, demanded the right to answer Mirabeau. The Assembly, after a certain amount of altercation, voted to recognize Ricard; and at the end of his speech, the sitting was adjourned. On the second day of the debate, closure was pronounced over the protest of a minority which apparently assumed that three days would be devoted to the discussion. Mirabeau gave some evidence that he desired to speak, but he was estopped by the closure.

Whatever Mirabeau's intentions may have been in connection with the Brest incident debate, he had not changed his views about parliamentary government. This fact is clearly attested by his numerous "Notes for the Court." A little more than a month before the debate on the Menou report, he stressed to the king the importance of harmonious relations between the king and the Assembly, insisting that the ministers were the proper instrumentality for securing such harmony and again regretting the decree of the previous November, which excluded the ministers from the Assembly and members of the Assembly from the Ministry. Concerning the ministers he asserted to the king:

Their presence alone can serve as intermediary and as common bond between the powers, which it is easier to separate in theory than in practice. In that way, all active measures of the legislative body would appear to be merely measures of the executive authority. Two opposing goals would not be presented to the people for their respect; there would be unity of action in authority. The National Assembly would increase its true force, and the king would maintain his prerogative. If this arrangement is always indispensable in the form of government that we have adopted, it is still more so in a moment of revolution, in which the royal authority, shaken in every part and paralyzed in all its energies, may perish either through inaction or through the competition of another authority, which would need, in order to replace it, only to be supported by circumstances.

With all this in mind, Mirabeau, knowing that the Menou report was impending, felt that much importance attached to avoiding the shock to royal authority which he conceived a vote of no confidence in the ministers would be. His advice therefore was that the king should immediately dismiss the ministers. "What would save everything," he wrote, "would be to get, in anticipation of the decree, the resignation of the ministers, and to appoint a new Ministry, formed in accordance with impulsion from the majority and supported by it. That alone is the solution of the difficulty." Mirabeau repeated the assertion several times. He did not hesitate to suggest that it might even be desirable to take ministers from the Jacobin Club. According to his famous dictum, "Minister Jacobins would not be Jacobin ministers." Again, even after the defeat of the Menou proposal, he was in a day or two still insisting to the king:

Is the wish that of governing? It is possible only through the majority; and the majority can be influenced only by getting close to it, by giving it the Ministry that appears suitable to it, by forcing it to defend it, and by causing it to be mollified through the inevitable effect of reciprocal confidence.

The king did not heed the advice of Mirabeau to dismiss the ministers in anticipation of a vote of no confidence. When a division on the Menou proposal was taken in the Assembly

on 20 October, Mirabeau cast his vote for the proposal. However, owing to a somewhat complicated political situation,
the Right being in opposition out of regard for royal authority and part of the Left being friendly to the Ministers,
the Menou proposal was defeated by a vote of 403 to 440.[18]

On 21 October, in spite of the vote the previous day on
the Menou proposal, four of the ministers addressed a letter
to the king, suggesting their retirement. In this letter, they
reminded the king that he had chosen them from the Assembly, which had expressed its gratitude for the choice,
asserting that it would have made the same selection. The
ministers went on to say that this support from the Assembly
was necessary, but that, inasmuch as they no longer had the
confidence of the whole Assembly, the king ought to consider
the question of supplanting them. The next day, the king
replied that he was deeply touched and would take the matter
under consideration. On the day after that, La Luzerne,
Minister of Marine,[19] feeling that the connection of the
proposed vote of no confidence with the disorders at Brest
involved him particularly, tendered his resignation. This was
accepted by the king with expressions of regret.[20]

In the first week of November, the forty-eight sections of
the Municipality of Paris convened for the purpose of discussing the question of dismissal of the unpopular ministers.
On 10 November a deputation from Paris, with Bailly at its

[18] Before the vote was taken, the Assembly had adopted an amendment expressly excepting Montmorin, Minister of Foreign Affairs,
from the vote of no confidence. This was distasteful both to the
opponents of Montmorin and to the friends of the other ministers.

[19] In point of fact, he was not, it will be recalled, chosen from
the Assembly, but was Minister of Marine at the outbreak of the
Revolution.

[20] His successor was Claret de Fleurieu, an official of some experience, who was, of course, not a member of the National Assembly.

head and with Danton as its spokesman, was admitted before
the Assembly; and, in a disorderly sitting marked by inter-
ruptions from the Right, a petition from Paris was presented
asking the Assembly to demand from the king dismissal of
the ministers and arrangement for their trial.[21] However, the
Assembly took no steps to comply with the petition. Two
days later, the Keeper of the Seals [22] wrote a letter to the
Assembly in which he asserted that as a former member of
the Assembly he could not allow the Paris petition to pass
unnoticed. He demanded to know the specifications of the
charges against him. At the end of another ten days, he
dispatched another letter, stating that at the order of the king
he had resigned.

The king, who had meanwhile, appointed Duportail, a
friend of Lafayette's who had served with him in America,
in the place of La Tour du Pin Gouvernet, Comte de Paulin,
supplanted Champion de Cicé with another friend of Lafayette's, the Parisian lawyer Duport-du-Tertre. These two
new ministers both took occasion to communicate to the
National Assembly news of their appointment. In the course
of their communication, they paid tribute to the Revolution
and to the National Assembly, stressing their desire to conduct themselves in conformity with the will of the Assembly.
Duvergier de Hauranne, appraising the situation from the
point of view of parliamentary government, not unnaturally
holds that action had come too late to do good.[23]

[21] Comte de Paulin, Minister of War, had resigned on the previous
day.

[22] Champion de Cicé.

[23] *Op. cit.*, I, 102: "L'acte qui, en temps utile, eût pu être un gage
de bonne intelligence, entre le roi et la majorité de l'Assemblée,
devint ainsi un acte de faiblesse, et le signe visible de l'abaissement
de la royauté."

VII

The Constitution before the Assembly: The Question of the Status of Ministers

IN the last part of the year 1790 and the earlier part of the year 1791, the period to which a French historian has given the title "The Crisis of the Revolution," [1] the history of the National Assembly followed the same general lines that characterized the activity of that body at the end of 1789 and the beginning of 1790. The Assembly continued to divide its attention between formulation of various parts of the Constitution and efforts to grapple with disorders and with other problems of current government, particularly those which were financial in character. In the period, the principal event that had relevance for the problem of parliamentary government was consideration by the Assembly, beginning in March of 1791, of the provisions concerning organization of the Ministry proposed to be introduced into the Constitution.

Louis XVI had bitterly resented the necessity of changing his ministers. The new choices were in reality those of Lafayette, not of himself. The king had by this time definitively

[1] Madelin, *Les Hommes de la Révolution*, pt. I, ch. viii.

gone over to counterrevolution. He was determined upon flight. Meanwhile, the National Assembly, under the direction of the Left, had more and more consolidated its position as possessor in fact of supreme legal power. With some reason it came to regard the ministers as the subservient agents of its will. In other words, there came to exist in the Assembly a situation, approved by the Left, which represented a definite tendency toward what has come to be called *gouvernement d'assemblée.*[2] In these conditions, the Assembly proceeded to consider what provisions concerning ministerial organization it would incorporate into the future Constitution of France.

Report by the Committee on the Constitution: March, 1791

On 7 March 1791 the order of the day in the National Assembly called for presentation of a report by the Committee on the Constitution concerning organization of the Ministry. The reporter on behalf of the committee was one of its original members, Desmeuniers. The report was followed by a draft measure consisting of thirty-three articles.

The Desmeuniers report began promisingly enough. Employing terminology that has since been reproduced throughout Europe[3] in written monarchical constitutions, it said:

The person of the king shall be inviolable and sacred. Through a happy fiction, it is assumed that the king, acting in the capacity of chief of the general administration, always wills the good; and he thus presents through himself no guarantee. But, as political institutions ought to be based on solid foundations, a

[2] Cf. Conclusion, pp. 240–241.
[3] E.g., in France, Italy, the Netherlands, and Scandinavia. In France, the concept was vigorously debated in 1791 following the flight of the king on 20 June. Cf. Ch. IX, pp. 201–204.

constitutional provision should stipulate that the executive authority will act, in the matter of administration, only through the intermediary of several agents, called ministers, who will answer for all public acts of the king.

Having thus correctly stated the principle underlying parliamentary government, Desmeuniers at once revealed that he was thinking in terms of the legal, not the political, position of ministers. He spoke of the problem "of confining within the boundaries of law all acts of the government." The kind of system that he envisaged was clearly one based on a rigid interpretation of the doctrine of the separation of powers. "It was," declared his report to the Assembly, "by early following the great principle of the division of the political powers that you have overcome all obstacles—the principle which has guided you up to this point and which will guide you until the end of your career." The inspiration of the report and of the proposal was the apparently ineradicable traditional distrust of ministers. "The precautions," asserted the report, "which guarantee the rights of citizens against usurpation by the Ministry are greatly multiplied in the plan."

So far as the plan itself was concerned, the committee attempted, by an impossibly rigid classification, to deal solely with the matter of ministerial organization, to the exclusion of important related and interrelated questions. The problem of function, for example, was recognized only insofar as was necessary for purposes of outlining the structure of the Ministry. Thus, after an initial article stipulating that "to the king alone shall belong the appointment and the removal of ministers," the thirteen following articles were concerned with establishment of the six ministries—Justice, Interior, Colonies, War, Navy, and Foreign Affairs—into which the executive branch of government was by the plan divided.

One article stipulated that the six ministers should compose the King's Council; but the same provision, strikingly enough, declared "there shall be no prime minister" (Art. XXVII). Authorization was granted for Orders in Council to be issued (Art. XIV); and the Council was given power to authorize on certain conditions extraordinary expenditure (Art. XVIII). The general spheres of activity of the individual ministers was defined in the thirteen articles which established the several ministries. At the same time, a few special articles were concerned with the specific problem of maintaining order in the country (Arts. XXII–XXVI). Stipulation was made for salaries (Art. XXVII) and, on certain conditions, pensions (Art. XXXIII) for the individual ministers. The relation of the ministers to the king was, in accordance with the opening statement of the report, arranged in the manner traditional for parliamentary government. That is to say, all orders of the king and all Orders in Council were to require for validity countersignature by a minister (Art. XVI). The following article established the English stipulation that no minister could plead an order of the king (Art. XVII).[4]

Employment of the concept of countersignature at this time deserves brief comment perhaps. In France, as on the continent of Europe generally, a stipulation for countersignature in connection with constitution drafting has, as is not surprising, become in some sort symbolic of the English parliamentary system. It is probably natural that a drafter who is not British, in seeking a specific aspect of a highly intangible relationship, should settle on countersignature.[5] In France, the phenomenon is by no means a recent one, some

[4] Ministers were also forbidden to plead an Order in Council.
[5] Cf., e.g., A. Lawrence Lowell, *The Government of England* (new ed.; New York, 1912), I, 29–31.

evidence suggesting that a linking of responsibility with countersignature goes back to the reign of Philippe IV (1285–1314).[6] So far as the Revolution is concerned, Mirabeau, who displayed striking understanding of the political responsibility of ministers, not unnaturally had some feeling for the importance of countersignature. For example, on 5 October 1789 he had said in the National Assembly in the course of debate: "The answer of the king is not countersigned by a minister. It ought to be; for otherwise the salutary principle of responsibility will always be eluded."[7] Mirabeau expressed almost identical sentiments in financial debate on 26 March 1790. The example of the French Constitution of 1791, together with the Constitution of Imperial Germany and a number of others, not to mention practice in the United States, shows abundantly what reason suggests, that countersignature in itself will not establish the relationship of parliamentary government. What would seem to be the case is this: if a chief executive whose decisions require countersignature is as responsible as those who sign, he may remain a *real* executive, making his own decisions; whereas, if the chief executive is irresponsible and the signers responsible, no self-respecting signer will *in the long run* serve unless the actual decision is his own.

All the remaining articles presented by Desmeuniers were concerned with the relations of the ministers to the legislature. Upon the ministers was imposed the obligation of making recommendations concerning desirable legislation (Art. XV). They were required to make reports to the legislature, especially in the matter of expenditure, whenever the

[6] This is the conviction of L. Perrichet, *La Grande Chancellerie de France* (Paris, 1912). The *dictionnaires, répertoires*, etc., suggest merely that countersignature was introduced by Louis XII (1498–1515).

[7] Cf. Sagnac in Lavisse, *Histoire de France contemporaine*, I, 101.

legislature might require (Art. XIX). Moreover, express provision was made that "the legislative body shall have power to present to the king such addresses as it shall judge fitting concerning the conduct of his ministers" (Art. XXVIII). Such stipulations, it seems clear, formed a basis for political responsibility, though they did not, of course, of necessity ensure full development of this kind of relationship, as it exists under parliamentary government. However, the responsibility that was envisaged was manifestly legal responsibility. The article which declared that "the ministers shall be responsible to the legislative body" immediately specified the occasions on which this responsibility would come into operation (Art. XX). Responsibility was to extend "(1) to all acts which should be injurious to national security, the Constitution, and the laws, (2) to every outrage to the liberty and the property of citizens, and (3) to all cases of waste of public funds which they might have part in or might facilitate." One article stipulated that action could not be taken against a minister without authority of a specific statute (Art. XXXIX), and two others regulated certain details of such action (Arts. XXX and XXXI). Otherwise, responsibility, it was stipulated, would be regulated in its details, including those concerning penalties, by a separate statute (Art. XXI).

Desmeuniers recognized in his report that the plan for ministerial organization which had been presented was a narrow one. Proposals so limited in scope had, he suggested, been determined upon in order that delicate questions might be avoided. "Thus, for example," ran the report, "we shall not examine whether the ministers may be members of the legislative body." [8] In other words, a question which Mi-

[8] This is taken from a short paragraph which is found in the report as given in *Arch. parl.*, XXIII (7 March 1791), 716, but not in the *Moniteur*, 1791, no. 67 (7 March), p. 274.

rabeau had insisted to be vital for political responsibility involved for Desmeuniers merely the kind of legal responsibility which doctrinaire advocates of the separation of powers had so much discussed. In this connection, one passage from the Desmeuniers report was of no little interest in its bearing on the problem of parliamentary government:

A sort of discredit has become prevalent concerning the expression *responsibility*. This bias is the result of a confusion of ideas. It seems that each task, each action of the minister who acts in good faith and according to his lights, exposes him to a penalty. Such a servitude is with reason regarded as impossible and illusory; but, I repeat, it is a pure confusion of ideas. Incapacity or negligence which is not the result of bad intention and which, even with suspect or bad intentions, is confined to a passive role can expose a minister only to public disfavor or to a petition by the legislative body which warns the king of the impotence or of the bad will of his agent. Responsibility is wholly another thing. It is exercised in connection with actions. It subjects to a penalty every minister who permits himself any act whatever against the Constitution and the laws, against the libery and the property of citizens, who permits himself or facilitates misappropriation of state funds. These three bases of responsibility will be developed elsewhere. Wishing here only to dissipate an error, we confine ourselves to the distinction which we have just established.[9]

Debate concerning Adjournment

Inasmuch as the narrow character of the Desmeuniers proposals was recognized by the committee report itself, omissions in them were seized upon by certain members as a basis for criticism and as the foundation ultimately for a motion to adjourn debate on the proposals. Such discussion

---

[9] Here, again, the passage is found in the *Archives* but not in the *Moniteur*.

as took place when the reading of the report and of the articles that were attached to it had been concluded was brief. Debate was concerned mainly with the motion for adjournment and very little with the merits of the proposals themselves. Only half a dozen speakers were reported as having taken part. Of these only one, Le Chapelier, opposed adjournment. He protested against what he considered constant adjournment of serious questions. He recognized that the proposals under discussion needed amendment, but he thought they formed a sufficient basis for discussion. The consensus for adjournment was due, as Barnave suggested, to a variety of motives. Cazalès agreed. He was, like Barnave, in favor of adjournment, but his reasons were of course entirely different. Mirabeau also supported adjournment, asserting that the proposals of the committee could properly be discussed only in connection with the matter of ministerial responsibility. The Assembly thereupon adjourned debate on the committee proposals. The questions involved were brought up for discussion a month later. Meanwhile, Mirabeau had died on 2 April.

Debate on the Report: Republican Tendencies

Debate on the matter of the organization of the Ministry was initiated in the National Assembly on 6 April. Discussion continued for several days. Much of the debate was only indirectly related to the problem of parliamentary government, and yet some aspects of the discussion, more particularly on the opening day, were in this respect both interesting and instructive.

The debate on 6 April was once more inaugurated by the committee reporter, Desmeuniers. He began by reminding the Assembly of its action, a month before, in adjourning debate on the committee's proposals. The Assembly had apparently been influenced by two omissions which it felt it detected in the committee report. The first was the failure of the committee to present details about the operation of the legal responsibility of the ministers, and the other was the silence of the report with respect to the matter of the presence of the ministers in the legislature. On the present occasion, the committee again failed to deal with the second matter. According to the reporter, the committee felt that the Assembly could not properly decide the question until it began its discussion, at an early date, of the organization of the legislature. On the other hand, with respect to the first question, the committee was of the opinion that the situation in the matter of details concerning ministerial offenses, of penalties for them, and of accusation was sufficiently satisfactory for discussion of ministerial organization to begin. The first two topics were, it was announced, treated in detail in a section of the projected penal code, which would soon be ready; whereas the subject of accusation was closely connected with that of the National High Court, which had recently been established in the course of formulation of the provisions regulating the judicial system.[10]

The Committee on the Constitution proposed to begin discussion on ministerial organization with the committee's original first draft article. This article recognized the power of appointment and removal to belong exclusively to the king. In the debate, no sooner had the article been presented to the Assembly than objections to its provisions arose. Robespierre, who was known to favor election of the principal executive agents, asserted amid much interruption that the Assembly was not prepared to discuss the question. He based his opinion on what he alleged to be a tendency on the part of the Assembly to proceed too hastily. He was of

[10] See *Moniteur*, 1791, no. 40 (9 Feb.), p. 163.

the opinion that the committee proposals vested so much power in the ministers as to warrant the fear that liberty would suffer from precipitate action. Charles de Lameth, while not opposing the article, contended that it ought not to be voted until the provisions concerning ministerial responsibility had been passed. He supported his contention concerning the order of procedure by the somewhat curious argument that if the Archbishop of Bordeaux, on the occasion when the vote of no confidence failed to pass in the Assembly, had remained in the Ministry, the counterrevolution would thereby have been rendered successful. His meaning seemed to be that only luck on the side of free government had enabled its cause to avoid disaster and that, for the future, the king must not be recognized to have full power to appoint and to remove—or not to remove—ministers, until specific provisions should be established whereby a minister could be removed regardless of the will of the king. Otherwise, the king, in accordance with the Assembly's own vote, could, he insisted, continue indefinitely in office a minister like the Archbishop of Bordeaux.

The next speaker, another member of the extreme Left, Pétion, representative of Chartres, supported the proposal that discussion of the article should be adjourned, agreeing with Robespierre that a precipitate decision was to be avoided. However, whereas Robespierre had not explicitly admitted his hostility to the article and whereas Charles de Lameth had stated that he was not opposed to it, Pétion frankly disapproved vesting in the king power of appointment and removal. His argument was based on a highly formal logical application of the concept of agency. In principle, the consequences of offenses committed by an agent are, he urged, visited upon the principal, who is responsible. The ministers are agents of the king, and yet he is recognized not to be responsible, this being an exception to principle; whereas the ministers are responsible for offenses of lesser officials, who are agents of the ministers. He urged that, to avoid the exception, the relation of the ministers to their principal, the king, ought to be made as regular as the relation of their subordinates to them. The means he advocated was to deprive the king of the power of appointment and to recognize that the ministers were "men of the nation." Pétion expressed himself as likewise favoring a definite term of office for the ministers, warning his hearers against putting much trust in responsibility, which he denominated "a feeble recourse." He contended that ministers who remained for a long time in office were, like all men, corrupted by the "habit of power," always becoming tyrants and oppressors. Many expedients, he asserted, existed by which responsibility could be escaped and by which the Constitution could be secretly undermined. Existence of such means was proved by the small number of ministers who had been impeached. The important thing, concluded Pétion, was method of choice.

Issue with Pétion's forthright position was joined by Le Chapelier, who asserted that he saw no reason for opposition to an article which recognized that the king possessed the power of appointment and removal. This article, he insisted, differentiated a monarchical system from a republic. Election of ministers for a fixed term was characteristic, he suggested, of a republican system, a consideration which ought to dispose of the arrangement as a basis for opposition to the committee's first article, because general agreement persisted on the maintenance of monarchy. The speaker, however, did not oppose adjournment, so long as the understanding prevailed that appointment and removal by the king constituted the true monarchical principle.

Interestingly enough, this discussion of royal appointment of ministers was one of the first occasions on which Robespierre's and Pétion's advocacy of a republican form of government was manifest. As a matter of fact, the general lines of constitutional development had for some time past been basically inconsistent with the maintenance of monarchy. More particularly, increasing certainty that a rigid separation of powers would prevail meant that the monarchical system was doomed.

The somewhat imponderable considerations which favor the existence of monarchy in modern times—matters of tradition, of sentiment, of prestige, and the like—are such that they inevitably tend to lose their force when the traditional position of the monarch is expressly and manifestly restricted by law. Intangible sources of strength are weakened by the very fact of being touched. Monarchy, combined with political democracy, must, it is true, be limited monarchy; but the limits cannot be the same in kind as the principles which determine the existence and character of monarchy. If political democracy is established in such a way that constitutional limitations, which must exist, take a form that is primarily legal, the system will of necessity be republican in character. This is, of course, precisely the identification that has now come to prevail in France. But inasmuch as political democracy has also come to be identified with parliamentary government in that country, the considerations just set out are of elementary but paramount significance in connection with the parliamentary system that was established with the Third Republic. The framing of the first Revolutionary Constitution thus forms an interesting part of the background of that system.

A majority of the framers of the Constitution of 1791 were determined narrowly to limit the executive power. They thereupon decided, with no little logic on their side, to limit the power of the king rigidly. Only those who had some feeling for the nature of parliamentary government understood that the statesmanlike, if less logical, procedure was not to limit the executive power by limiting the king but to limit the king by limiting the executive power. Thus, Le Chapelier was correct in asserting that to deprive the king of the power of appointment and removal was consistent with a republic, not with a monarchy. Choice of ministers for a fixed term by the voters or by the legislature is an arrangement which from the nature of the case must involve legal responsibility operating through impeachment. Such an arrangement may, of course, be established under a system that is called monarchy, but the arrangement is essentially republican in character. So also, an arrangement of this sort renders parliamentary government practically impossible. This is merely to say that monarchy which is worthy of the name can exist in combination with political democracy only through employment of the parliamentary system of government.

The converse of this proposition, however, involves considerations that are slightly more complex. Political democracy is, of course, perfectly compatible with republican government. Indeed, the view has, it may be repeated, long prevailed in France that the two are to be identified. The same, of course, is in general true of the United States. Political democracy, in American experience, has flourished in the absence of parliamentary government. Since, however, in France and on the continent of Europe, political democracy is traditionally associated with the parliamentary system, France inevitably developed under the Third Republic a system that was both republican and parliamentary. This somewhat unnatural combination has caused the government

of a French Republic not only to be basically different from
that of the American Republic but also to differ, though not
so greatly, from the parliamentary system in England and
from such European parliamentary systems as those of the
Netherlands, Belgium, and the Scandinavian countries. Certain characteristics of the parliamentary system that were
developed under the Third Republic and that prevailed under
the Fourth Republic, such, for example, as the "omnipotence"
of parliament, the essentially subordinate position of the
ministers, the paramount importance of committees, and the
antipathy for dissolution, received a fairly complete development during the life of the National Assembly of 1789. But
these characteristics, serving under the Third and Fourth
Republics merely to modify parliamentary government to
the point of becoming a French variant that is for the time
being in marked contrast with what is projected for the Fifth
Republic, were, in the early years of the Revolution, instru-
mental in preventing parliamentary government from being
established at all. The issue was, it would seem, less one between parliamentary and nonparliamentary government than
between monarchy and republic.

Debate on the Report: Ministerial Responsibility

Inasmuch as none of the members of the National Assembly who spoke on 6 April at the beginning of the debate on
ministerial organization were opposed to adjournment of discussion of the article that would vest power of appointment
and removal in the king, the Assembly without difficulty
decided to proceed at once to the matter of responsibility.
Accordingly, Desmeuniers read to the Assembly a series of
nine draft articles that the committee had grouped under the
heading *Responsibility*. In point of fact, this procedure
marked little apparent advance over the situation as it had

existed a month before, for the nine articles that were proposed at this time were nearly identical with articles that had been included at more than one point in the proposal as introduced in March. Thus, the first six articles on responsibility were, with only one exception, the same as six successive articles (Arts. XVI–XXI) contained in the body of the original proposal; and the last three articles of the later proposal were wholly identical with three articles found near the end of the earlier draft provisions. The one difference consisted of a provision stipulating, "The offenses, the damages, and the penalties that shall be pronounced against guilty ministers shall be determined in the penal code," this being substituted for an article reading, "The method of action in the matter of responsibility, the details of this responsibility, the damages and the penalties which may be pronounced against ministers who may have failed in their duties shall be determined by a special act."

The proposals concerning responsibility which were made by the Committee on the Constitution furnished further evidence of what was already abundantly clear—that the responsibility to which the majority of the Assembly were confining their attention was legal responsibility. Indeed, though distinguishing accurately between legal and political responsibility in his original report, Desmeuniers had refused, as has been seen, to apply the term *responsibility* to any but the first kind. Political responsibility, however, inevitably appeared to be present in the minds of such members as displayed real interest in practical governmental affairs.[11] Thus, no little significance would seem to attach to the fact that,

[11] This is, of course, the basic situation under the American system. It explains the fairly frequent outbursts of displeasure with heads of departments in the form of assertions that such heads ought to be impeached.

as soon as the committee proposals had been read to the
National Assembly, the discussion at once concerned itself
with responsibility of the political variety.

The first speaker in the debate on the committee proposals
was Menou. His comment was simple and clear, bearing on
a single point, illustrated by a concrete example. He complained that the ministers, under the proposed stipulations,
would not be responsible for the appointments which they
themselves would make. He referred particularly, he said, to
recent appointments made by Montmorin, Minister of Foreign Affairs. He stated that, as a member of the Committee
on Diplomacy, he had made representations to the minister
concerning his "most extraordinary choice," urging, he
interestingly enough related, that the persons appointed were
not strong supporters of the Revolution. In other words,
Menou's reasons were political in character, and the problem
to which he called attention lent itself to solution through
political much more than through legal responsibility. Indeed, the efficacy of criticism that is political in character,
even in the absence of parliamentary government, is illustrated by the fact that Montmorin on the next day wrote to
the National Assembly a long letter defending his appointments and, at the end, justifying his intention to retain his
position as long as he continued to receive the confidence of
the king.

The next speaker, another member of the extreme Left,
Buzot, representative of Evreux, took up the matter precisely
where Menou left off. "There are," he asserted, "many circumstances in which responsibility cannot be exercised in an
active manner"; and he maintained that, in such instances, the
influence of the legislature was all that remained. Buzot's
reason for pointing out the fact that legal responsibility
would not reach a case like that cited in connection with

appointments by the Minister of Foreign Affairs was, he said, that he wished to call attention to an omission in the proposed articles on responsibility. What he regretted to see left out was "the previous article that granted the legislative body the faculty of demanding of the king the dismissal of the ministers." Desmeuniers intervened merely to exclaim, "It was hooted"; but Buzot urged restoration of the article. He was supported by three other speakers—Charles de Lameth, Goupil de Préfeln, and the liberal noble, Beaumetz, representative of Artois. Goupil de Préfeln wished to go so far as to deal specifically with a situation in which the king might keep a minister in whom the legislature had declared it had no confidence, but Beaumetz opposed this on sound principles of parliamentary government. "In proportion," he said near the beginning of his speech, "as we acquire the practice of representative government, we shall distinguish legitimate accusations from declamations." And, near the end of his speech, he added: "I repeat that when we have acquired the practice of representative government, we shall know that it is impossible for a minister marked with the seal of national reprobation to continue in office." Thereupon, Desmeuniers, on behalf of the committee, readily assented to the proposal:

We see with pleasure that demand is made for restoration of Article XXVIII of our former plan. It had appeared to be rejected the first time because, so it was said, the provision expressed a right so incontestable that there was no use in mentioning it.[12] It is proper to observe that when you employed the right yourselves, there were many members in this Assembly who contested it.

[12] In the discussion in March which resulted in postponement of the debate on ministerial organization, Barère had, in alluding to specific objections to the committe proposals, stated that no necessity existed for reducing to writing the right of addressing the king.

In the debate at this time concerning restoration of the article that recognized the legislative right to address the king, such opposition as appeared was not based on principle. Adverse reaction proceeded from the less extreme Right, being clearly inspired by the prevailing one-sided tendency in the Assembly toward continual weakening of executive power. Thus, Cazalès, when Buzot had made his proposal, did not directly express hostility to it, contenting himself with saying that he did not know what "moral responsibility" was, that he did not know the meaning of "an anticonstitutional appointment when it falls on men who have taken the civic oath," and that his fixed belief was in the necessity for an "independent executive power." Later, when the committee through Desmeuniers offered to accept reinsertion of the article under discussion, Cazalès suggested that action be postponed until the article which was proposed could be debated in connection with the powers of the executive. In this way, he returned to a matter which he knew to be of paramount importance in connection with parliamentary government, the question of the power of dissolution. Cazalès said:

You by no means want the executive power to be dependent on the legislative power; and yet that is what would happen if the article should pass in the form in which it is proposed. The principle appears obvious to me. Every time that the legislative body speaks to kings in the name of the people, the kings are obliged to obey. But it is important that the legislative body should not express a will which is not that of the people. There exists a way to determine it. It is that of granting to the king the power of dissolving the legislature. (*Murmurs on the Left.*) This assertion excites murmurs. I shall, nevertheless, have the honor, when the question of completion of the executive power is raised, to make such a proposal, requiring at the same time that the king shall take the necessary precautions for convening another legislature at once and shall accept its will. If the Assembly is willing to grant me a moment of silence, I shall prove that there is no liberty, no public prosperity, unless the king has this right.

Montlosier, proceeding along the same lines, pretended that he had a proposal which would bring all parties into agreement, causing amusement by suggesting adoption of a stipulation "that it shall be permitted to the king to make a proclamation couched in these terms: *'I declare that the legislature no longer has the confidence of the nation.'*" The Assembly, however, was in no mood to heed this true word spoken in jest. Its position was put by Le Chapelier:

It is not at a time that the Constitution is being established and that the first legislature is going to have to defend it against attacks which may be brought against it that we should grant to the king the right to dissolve it. There might as well be granted to him that of destroying the Constitution.

When discussion had been closed concerning the right of address, the Assembly adopted an article couched in the following terms: "The legislative body shall have power to present to the king such declarations as it shall judge suitable concerning the conduct of the ministers and even to declare to him that they have lost the confidence of the nation." Article XXVIII of the original committee proposal had been worded in almost identically the same terms as the first part of the article that was adopted. The second part of the article adopted was added by Desmeuniers. At this time, Robespierre declared his opposition to the word *address*, on the ground that it made the legislative body appear to speak like a petitioner; [13] and Prieur proposed and secured adoption

[13] The account is in the *Archives* but not in the *Moniteur*.

of the word *declare*, asserting that the legislative body had
not only the power but the duty—failure to perform which
would constitute betrayal of the nation—to declare to the
king such truths as that the ministers had not the confidence
of the people.

Debate on the Report: Membership of Ministers in the Legislature

On the second day of the debate on ministerial organization, 7 April, one or two events occurred that were of some
relevance to the problem of parliamentary government. In
the first place, a proposal was made and adopted which, in
accordance with sentiment that had already more than once
manifested itself and had apparently been progressively
growing stronger, would introduce into the Constitution a
stipulation to the effect that the king could not take ministers
from the legislature. The proposal was made by Robespierre
at the opening of debate on the second day. He moved that
no member of the Assembly should be allowed to enter the
Ministry for a period of four years following the end of its
session. "A philosopher whose principles you honor," he
asserted, "said that the legislator, in order to inspire more
respect and confidence, ought to isolate himself from his
work." His proposal, Robespierre somewhat curiously alleged,[14] was an application of this principle. However that
might be, several members supported the proposal or even
suggested its extension.[15] The extensions suggested included

[14] Chevallier, in his *Barnave*, p. 234, suggests that this was a part
of Robespierre's persistent opposition to the "Triumvirate." Robespierre later made the same argument, it would seem with somewhat
more reason, with respect to advocacy of the proposition that members of the legislature should not be re-eligible. Cf. Ch. VIII, p. 191.

[15] Among the speakers were Bouché, Dandré, Pétion, Beaumetz,
Roederer, Le Boidaiguier, and Louis de Noailles.

application of the prohibition to members of future legislatures as well as to members of the National Assembly,
application of it to members of the high courts, prohibition
of military positions as well as of posts in the Ministry, prohibition of gifts, salaries, pensions, and the like, and establishment of penalties for violation of the prohibitions. These
suggestions of wholesale prohibition, which so clearly lend
themselves to burlesque, were treated by the elder Garat
with a flippancy that was possibly deserved. He said:

In order that the interests of the nation may not be betrayed
either directly or indirectly, the provision of the decree that
is proposed to you ought to be extended not only to representatives but to their ancestors, descendants, and collateral kin.
This is the only way of allowing the decree proposed to you
to prevail in all its purity.[16]

Among the members of the Assembly, Tracy was the only
deputy recorded as taking direct issue with the Robespierre
and related proposals. This representative of the nobility
from Moulins insisted that the proposals presented certain
"disadvantages," protesting that his motives could not be
impugned, inasmuch as he sought no position and was confident no position would seek him. His fundamental objection to the proposed prohibition was that it "reduces the
executive power to choosing its agents from among the persons whom it is least calculated to know, whereas its principal task is to make good choices."

Beaumetz, who spoke after Tracy in the debate and who
in a measure spoke in direct reply to him, afforded an excellent example of the attitude of distrust of authority that
prevailed so widely in the eighteenth century. Abundant
evidence could be found that this attitude characterized a

[16] For similar ridiculing of a similar proposal, cf. Ch. VIII, p. 187.

substantial majority of the members of the National Assembly. It was an attitude that manifested itself in France toward government in general and, as has been several times stressed, toward ministers in particular. Thus, Beaumetz' appeal was not to reason but to fear. He argued that sentiment, not logic, should prevail. "When one follows the dictate of one's heart," he asserted, "one is sure not to be deceived. Even if the proposals which are offered should have disadvantageous results, could they counterbalance the danger of infecting members of the legislature with intrigue?"

The voting of the Robespierre and related proposals was a foregone conclusion. A suitable combination of the several stipulations which had been suggested was agreed upon. It was worded as follows:

The National Assembly decrees constitutionally that its members and those of future legislatures, as well as members of the Tribunal of Cassation, shall not be eligible, for a period of four years after having ceased the exercise of their functions, to be appointed to the Ministry, or to receive from the executive power or its agents any employment, places, gifts, gratuities, salaries, or commissions of any kind. No member of the legislative body shall solicit any office or favors from the government or the agents of the executive power either for another or for himself. The Committee on the Constitution shall propose the penalty to be visited on those who shall contravene the present decree.

With the voting of Robespierre's resolution, the debate on ministerial responsibility was momentarily interrupted. The break was made in order that pertinent sections of the projected penal code might be read. Provisions of this document concerned with responsibility were announced on behalf of the combined Committees on the Constitution and Criminal Legislation, by one of the reporters, Lepelletier, representative of Paris, to be contained in that part of the code which dealt with misdemeanors calculated "to compromise the public interest." So far as ministers were concerned, the basic assumption was that "the capacity of minister," far from being a "certificate of impunity," was a reason "for pronouncing graver penalties against ministers than against other public functionaries, and against functionaries than against ordinary private individuals." The offenses which it was contemplated the ministers might commit were listed under three rubrics. The first class consisted of offenses against the external safety of the state. The second class consisted of offenses against the Constitution. In the third class were placed offenses which ministers might commit in their capacity as public servants. The nature of the various specific offenses listed made it abundantly clear that the responsibility which was envisaged was far from being the kind of answerability for general policy which responsibility in the context of parliamentary government has come to have. The severity of the proposed penalties reflected the disrepute into which ministers had fallen. More often than not the established penalty was capital punishment [17] or penal servitude for life. For example, the death penalty, to choose at random, was established for a minister who should publish a designedly falsified law, and the same severity was to be visited on a minister who should countersign an act calculated to delegate authority contrary to the Constitution.

Debate on the Report: Administrative Reorganization

The provisions on ministerial responsibility having, with knowledge of the pertinent provisions of the penal code as

[17] A proviso was added that if the Assembly should decide to abolish the death penalty, then whatever was established in its place should be substituted in the stipulations concerning the pertinent ministerial offenses.

a background, been determined by the National Assembly, the Assembly proceeded to deal successively with the several remaining articles concerning the Ministry that had been proposed by the committee. The discussion, which inevitably assumed a somewhat anticlimactic character, extended over some four or five days, though the final vote on the provisions concerning the Ministry was, owing to delay caused by the necessity for the committee to study several additional articles proposed on the floor and referred to it, not taken for about three weeks.

The debate was at all times guided by Desmeuniers with no little skill. He was confronted with a situation in which relatively unimportant matters were the occasion for long-winded speeches, whereas more momentous provisions were, in the laconic phraseology of the official reports, voted "almost without discussion." The list of particular ministries suggested by the committee was approved in slightly modified form, and the distribution of functions, with the adjustments consequent upon the modification, was accepted.

In the course of these proceedings, issue was joined somewhat vigorously between Right and Left concerning the proper basis of authority for deciding upon executive structure and distribution of functions. In general, the Left argued strongly that decision in these matters should be made by legislative enactment, whereas the Right was convinced that determination should belong largely to the executive. Thus, for probably the first time in European history, this subject, frequently discussed since, was debated.

The traditional argument, so largely influential on the continent of Europe, that democratic theory can be satisfied to leave administrative organization to the executive as long as control of expenditure remains firmly in the hands of the representatives of the people, would seem basically to violate British and American views somewhat less than might at first sight appear. The executive in Britain can, it seems not inaccurate to say, confidently anticipate approval by Parliament of any alterations in structure it advocates; and Congress, when it faces facts, recognizes that no extensive administrative reorganization is practicable except through legislative ratification of plans formulated by the executive. France, in 1920, seemed to reverse its traditional practice by stipulating specific statutory authorization for modification of structure, but habit was apparently often too strong for this requirement to receive regular compliance.

In the debate in the National Assembly, the flair of members for lengthy doctrinaire speeches found in the subject of administrative organization a congenial basis for elaborate argument. Inasmuch as all were agreed that in principle the final word was with the legislature, the question was, as it would seem to continue to be,[18] how much, if any, initial determination by the executive is consistent with the principle. The position of the Left, that the number and functions of ministries should be regulated in detail by statutory provisions, was doubtless, in formal logic, a natural one for members who were convinced that legal limitation was a better safeguard against a distrusted corruptible executive than was the less precisely defined operation of the political responsibility characteristic of parliamentary government. In any case, the rigid logical view, ably presented by Barnave, was victorious.

[18] See, e.g., L. Duguit, *L'Organisation politique de la France* (Paris, 1924), pp. 720–721.

VIII

The Constitution before the Assembly: The Question of the Legislature

THE order of the day for 16 May in the National Assembly called for discussion of proposals by the Committee on the Constitution concerning the structure and functions of the legislative body. On behalf of the committee, Thouret presented a report to accompany the text of ninety-nine draft articles offered for the Assembly's approval. The report contained a minimum of argument, being confined largely to explanatory classification of the large number of articles proposed. The reporter estimated that some twenty-five of the draft articles had already been voted. Consideration by the Assembly of the remainder of the proposed provisions consumed seven consecutive days. Several articles were recommitted, a final vote being taken on 13 June.

Thouret, in steering through the National Assembly the committee proposals concerning the legislative branch of government, displayed the skill of which he had already shown himself capable. His own interventions were cogently reasoned and clearly expressed, the tone of his arguments constituting a model which some of the speakers might have done well to emulate. The task of direction, it is not without interest to note, proved so exhausting that the reporter was on occasion compelled to have a colleague act as substitute for him.

The general pattern of the Assembly debate concerning proposals for the legislature was the familiar one that involved apparently inexhaustible ornate oratory concerning what appeared often to be relatively minor points, balanced by rapid passage of large blocks of draft articles, noted more than once in the official report as voted "almost without discussion" or "after a light discussion." Partisan divisions appeared more pronounced than ever. The extreme Left, especially, was conscious of the superior voting strength of the combination of which it was for the time a part, frequently interjecting into the procedure impatient demands for closure of discussion and calls for the question. Conditions outside the Assembly naturally exercised strong influence within. The prevailing atmosphere of suspicion and distrust continued strikingly evident.

Debate of the Committee Report:
Re-eligibility of Members

Thouret, when he had presented to the National Assembly the committee report, together with the draft articles on the legislative branch of government, initiated debate by reading two of the articles. The first declared eligible for election to the legislature the holders of various offices, including that of minister, provided the candidate should possess the requisite qualifications; and the second stipulated that members of the legislature should be indefinitely re-eligible. Discussion growing out of these two articles, which were taken in reverse order, consumed four out of the seven days devoted to consideration of all the proposals concerning the legislature.

Debate on the re-eligibility of members of the legislature was from the beginning conditioned by the fact that the committee favored re-eligibility as a principle, whereas most of the members of the National Assembly were clearly moved by a strong impulse to declare themselves ineligible for the legislature that was to be established by the Constitution. Touret's able plea for calm discussion of the whole question on principle was followed by a flood of rhetoric; and an impatient Assembly, at the end of its first day of debate, voted "almost unanimously" in favor of excluding its own members from the future legislature, the Assembly being reported as adjourning "amidst its own applause." Later, on 28 May, Roederer, though a member of the extreme Left, is recorded as suggesting that "the Assembly should decide that after the present session all its members will withdraw into a convent." Duvergier de Hauranne,[1] in an acute analysis of the situation, quotes Ferrières as follows: "Neither the Jacobins nor the Aristocrats wanted the Constitution; they had a common interest in excluding from the next Assembly the members of the existing Assembly."

On the three days following the decree to exclude members of the National Assembly from the next legislature, the question of re-eligibility in its more general form was debated. In spite of able support of the committee's position, especially by Thouret in opening and closing this part of the discussion, opposition to re-eligibility was strong; and, when the "pale liberal," Barère, representative of Bigorre, proposed that members of the legislature should be eligible to succeed themselves for only one consecutive term, his suggestion was adopted in the place of the committee draft

[1] *Op. cit.*, I, 182.

article. Thereupon Thouret read the first draft article, which had not been taken in its regular order. This proposal, it may be repeated, stipulated that the holding of public office did not in itself constitute ineligibility to election to the legislature. The reporter recognized that, so far as ministers were concerned, the question of eligibility was reciprocally connected with that of whether members of the legislature could be appointed to the Ministry. The Assembly, "after a slight discussion," approved Thouret's suggestion of accepting the draft article without prejudice as to its application to ministers, the difficult question of the converse of the stipulation to be adjourned.

Finally, Thouret, on 9 June, presented new proposals concerning the eligibility of officials. The text was the subject of much hairsplitting altercation, though the question of the ministers was not mentioned.[2] The draft article was so phrased at this time as to stipulate that certain fiscal and other administrative agents should, if elected to the legislature, be required to choose. Subsequently, the wording was altered so as expressly to mention the ministers. As a result of further drafting, the Assembly, on 3 June, adopted a text consisting of six articles.

The indefinite re-eligibility of elected representatives in legislatures is so unquestioningly accepted in free countries at the present day that some initial difficulty attaches to understanding the seemingly interminable oratory to which debate of the subject gave rise in the National Assembly. On the other hand, anyone possessed of the patience to attempt to extract from the lengthy speeches some of the principal arguments employed should perhaps be less surprised after finding that the debaters made efforts to come to grips with such concepts as national sovereignty, the sovereignty of the

[2] Cf. Ch. X, p. 210.

people, the nature of representative government, the true scope of liberty, the dangers of despotism and anarchy, and so on. Basic principles seemed often in conflict; but, even where principle could be agreed upon, similar agreement on the need for modification in application opened wide the field of disagreement concerning where the line was to be drawn. And behind the surface of the arguments was the bitterness of political factionalism in the country at large and in the Assembly. The members of the moderate constitutional party, under the leadership of the Committee on the Constitution, being pressed hard between the Right and the "advanced" and extreme Left and being met by vacillation and intrigue instead of leadership on the part of the court, were not without courage in supporting arrangements upon which they felt survival of monarchy and of stable government to depend.

Thouret and the committee, though overwhelmingly defeated through the impulsive quasi-unanimity with which the National Assembly voted to exclude its members from the first legislature, pressed for indefinite re-eligibility of the members of the legislature and of its successors. They received unexpected support from the Left in the person of the able member of the "Triumvirate," Adrien Duport, and from the Right in that of Cazalès. Duport's change of position was a manifestation of divisive tendencies among the Jacobins in the Assembly, of which other evidence was not lacking. Moreover, the situation reflected, of course, conditions on the outside. Certainly worthy of mention is the fact that Barnave [3] had recently succeeded, to the dismay

[3] Duvergier de Hauranne (*op. cit.*, I, 173) erroneously dates approval of this address as 18 May, in the midst, that is, of the debate in the Assembly. Actually, the date was some two months earlier. Cf. Aulard *La Société des Jacobins*, II, 185 ff.; Chevallier, *Barnave*, pp. 217–218, *Mirabeau*, p. 337.

of more extremist members, in having voted by the Paris society and circulated to all affiliated local societies an address
warning against the evils of "turbulence" and praising the
virtues and good intentions of Louis XVI.

Both Duport and Cazalès had voted for declaring the members of the National Assembly ineligible for the first legislature. Now, however, both insisted on the principle of
indefinite re-eligibility for the future as making for much-
needed strength and stability in government. Duport was
convinced that the national interest required the Left to regard the Revolution as accomplished, and hence to recognize
that to push further was to risk anarchy; Cazalès in the same
interest urged the Right to accept the Revolution as an accomplished fact, realizing that reaction and counterrevolution rendered impossible the salvaging of anything for the
cause of monarchy and tradition.

Thouret and the committee, in supporting re-eligibility in
the case of members both of the National Assembly and of
future legislatures, rested their principal argument squarely
on the fundamental right of the people to elect their representatives, and the same was true of Duport and Cazalès and
other supporters of re-eligibility, when the question became
confined to re-eligibility of members of future legislatures.
All insisted that non-re-eligibility was destructive of national
and popular sovereignty, as curtailing exercise of the only
authority which the nation, in not delegating, had reserved
to itself, namely, that of electing its representatives. Such
curtailment would likewise render the people impotent to
reward those who had deserved well of the country and to
secure, if they should desire, the aid of men who might have
gained worth-while experience.

Opponents of re-eligibility insisted in the beginning that
a distinction should be made between a constituent and a

legislative assembly, and then, starting from this wholly tenable position, they combined the somewhat self-righteous plea by Robespierre that the Assembly should show itself noble with the related contention that the Assembly should furnish no basis for future suspicion that it had ever subordinated the national to private interest. This was the kind of opposition that had gained the almost unanimous vote of frenzied self-abnegation. Thereafter, whereas advocates of re-eligibility contended that the issue had become simplified and clarified through elimination of any consideration of self-interest, opponents, who had insisted on the distinction between constituent and legislative bodies, did not hesitate to employ the somewhat circular argument that the Assembly had by its own high-minded action established the sound principle which ought consequently to be incorporated in the Constitution.

Perhaps the most subtle argument that was employed by the opponents of re-eligibility consisted of their references to examples. Such references were made not only to some examples already accepted by the National Assembly in France but also to those prevailing in England and the United States, namely, to instances of property,[4] age, and nationality qualifications and similar limitations. These, they contended, demonstrated clearly the need for modifying the principle of the unrestrained right of voting and electing. Concerning this point, the advocates themselves insisted, no

---

[4] Robespierre anticipated that he might be accused of inconsistency as having opposed a property qualification in the form of the famous "marc d'argent," but he argued that there was no difficulty in making a rational distinction, and he pressed on to accuse of inconsistency in this respect the advocates of re-eligibility. Some days later, on 28 May, Robespierre asserted that the time had come to reconsider the decision of the "marc d'argent," but he was unceremoniously shouted down.

doubt soundly but from the nature of things not very effectively, on distinctions. They argued that the burden of proof was on supporters of limitation, that any limitation should be absolutely necessary, and that such limitation should be general, as in the case of the exclusion of infants, and not personal, as in the case of the ineligibility of members of a given legislature.

Opponents of re-eligibility, as was scarcely surprising, invoked the catchwords of equality and liberty. They contended that the Assembly had already formulated essential aspects of a Constitution that was based on the abolition of aristocracy, and they accused the advocates of re-eligibility of undertaking insidiously to reintroduce aristocracy through an anticonstitutional proposal. The manifestations of the alleged revival of privileges which they professed to anticipate were intrigue and corruption. With more than one reference to what they conceived the situation in England to be, they asserted that long-continued power resulted in corruption; and re-eligibility was argued to be something greatly to be feared as likely to lead to precisely such corruption. The voters, being lazy, would tend to return the same members, especially key figures who had entered into intrigue with the executive authority. Hence the opponents of re-eligibility, while willing on occasion to accept the principle of the right of free election, urged the necessity for protection through limitation of the right in the name of liberty itself. Perhaps the most striking assertion of the applicability of equality and liberty in the matter was made by a somewhat retiring member of the first Committee on the Constitution, Larévellière-Lépeaux, representative of Anjou, who proclaimed that "all superiority, even of talents, is redoubtable for liberty." His own formula was this: "The people, far from destroying liberty, ensure it when through their representatives they impose upon themselves rules which preserve them from their own shortsightedness."

In general, each side made its case with an elaborateness of detail defying summary, and each remained unimpressed by the arguments of the other. The advocates of re-eligibility ridiculed arguments concerning corruption, endeavoring to bring the matter down from the realm of vague allegations to that of a definite practical problem; and the opponents were equally scornful of the need for re-election of men of experience, some of Robespierre's most sanctimonious modesty manifesting itself in assertions of his confident belief that the great French nation contained many able and selfless men equal on any count to members of the National Assembly.

Re-eligibility and Parliamentary Government

The debate in the National Assembly concerning re-eligibility of the members of legislatures would seem to have had little direct or immediate relevance to the problem of parliamentary government. The argument is doubtless tenable that, technically speaking, ministerial responsibility could conceivably prevail where members of the legislature are ineligible to succeed themselves. However, in connection with the problem of parliamentary government as a French problem of the moment, the debate in the National Assembly on re-eligibility was pertinent in an important, if somewhat negative, sense. In general, for the parliamentary system to have been established under a written constitution, favorable conditions would have been necessary at least to a certain extent. Approval would have had actually to exist of certain basic legal provisions, or in any case prevalence of disapproval would have had to be absent. Some support for the system and some understanding of it could not be out-weighed by hostility to it or by misunderstanding of it or by both. Such favorable conditions were proved by the debate to be far from general. They were indeed in what seems in retrospect progressive deterioration. This renders the persistence and the courage of the Committee on the Constitution, especially of members like Thouret, Desmeuniers, and Le Chapelier, the more remarkable.

That all the members of the Committee on the Constitution or even a majority of its membership, or that any substantial part of the committee's normal supporters or of its unexpected allies from the Right and Left, had a full understanding of parliamentary government may well be doubted. At the same time, they advocated institutional arrangements that would have furnished a suitable basis for the development of the parliamentary system. In consistently contending that the cause of true monarchy and of strong and stable government should and could be salvaged without damage to the accomplishments of the Revolution, they must have realized that they were advocating a reconciliation of certain forces through arrangements that would ultimately have to be worked out in practice or to work themselves out, even if these advocates could not possibly know fully that history was to show these arrangements to be inevitably those of the parliamentary system. The debate on re-eligibility was pertinent to the problem of parliamentary government at least insofar as it brought to light certain forces making for accomplishments which, if successful, would probably have worked in the right direction. Perhaps with a little luck their side might have prevailed against seemingly insuperable odds. However that might have been, the debate had a slight additional pertinence to the problem of parliamentary government. In the course of certain speeches, some allusion was made to two institutions that are well known to be closely interrelated with that system of government, namely, legislative control of the ministry and dissolution of the legislature.

Re-eligibility and Legislative Control of the Executive

When Thouret and several other advocates of re-eligibility emphasized the importance of not depriving a legislature of the experience of persons who had served well in a previous legislature, their argument was related by them in a simple way to the problem of ministerial responsibility, through the converse concept of legislative control. Thouret insisted that there must be recognized to exist "an eternal struggle" between legislature and executive and that the legislature, being the "sole shield" against the executive, had need of every asset "effectively to watch over it" on a plane of real equality with the branch of government which never failed to derive full advantage from its stability and continuity. Moreover, at least one speaker, Merlin, a noble elected by the Third Estate of Douai, placed the argument upon its fundamental principle and gave it sharp practical point through insistence on the special importance of possession by legislators of experience with public finance. In general, good will was, asserted Thouret, not enough; what was needed was knowledge.

Opponents of re-eligibility professed themselves as not much concerned about the problem of legislative control. Robespierre's confidence that plenty of good men would always be available to the country had the effect of waving the problem aside, and argument was even made [5] that an intriguing executive would actually be weakened through its inability to corrupt a legislature composed always of new members. But, fundamentally, the opponents were probably

[5] By Buzot, for example.

influenced principally by a rigidly doctrinaire belief that the separation of powers and legal responsibility were more effective safeguards than political control. "The true force of the legislative body," asserted Robespierre, "derives from the Constitution on which it is founded. . . . The power of the legislative body is immense by its very nature, and is guaranteed by its permanence, its right to assemble without call, and by the law which withholds from the king the right of dissolving it."

Re-eligibility and Dissolution

Robespierre's reference to dissolution is only one instance of the fact that the subject continued to rise from time to time during the debate. Members who appeared to have some feeling for the nature of parliamentary government understood clearly that dissolution was an institution which recognized the last word in national affairs to belong to the nation. These members, being leaders among the forces favoring the cause of re-eligibility, argued with impeccable logic that dissolution without re-eligibility would be absurd; but this of course was in fact far from proving that re-eligibility could not exist in the absence of dissolution; and non-re-eligibility, once adopted, destroyed, on their own logic, the case for dissolution. Opponents of re-eligibility had therefore from their point of view a somewhat simpler case. More than that, they insistently contended that dissolution was a formidable weapon in the hands of the executive; so that a recruit like Duport from the "Triumvirate" was constrained to argue that support of re-eligibility in no wise involved support of dissolution, the logic of which did not prevent Cazalès, an old supporter of dissolution, from imitating Thouret in extolling its merits without mentioning it by name. The Assembly, after deciding at the end of the long debate against indefinite re-eligibility, voted on the following day the article stipulating that "the king shall not have power to dissolve the legislative body." [6]

[6] The *Moniteur*, 1791, no. 142 (22 May), p. 590, records that this was Art. XXVIII, which was included along with Arts. X to XXXIV, inclusive, these being noted as passed "presque sans discussion" on 20 May. According to *Arch. parl.*, XXVI (20 May 1791), 250, the article was no. 30; and, in connection with it, a brief incident is recorded: "*M. Foucault-Lardivolie*. Je demande un léger changement. Au lieu de dire: Le roi ne pourra pas dissoudre la légisalture, c'est de dire: Le roi pourra dissoudre la législature (*Rires*) . . . et il sera tenu d'en convoquer une seconde. *A gauche:* Aux voix la question préalable sur le léger changement!" The Assembly is then recorded as rejecting the amendment and voting Art. 30.

IX

The Flight of the King: June, 1791

IF the members of the Committee on the Constitution, their supporters, and their allies displayed no little courage in fighting in May an almost hopeless battle in favor of a halt to the momentum of the Revolution and in favor of establishment of a firm position for the king and real strength for the executive, they required even greater courage for a task of apparently even less hope after the flight of the king on 20 June. Yet, they lost neither courage nor hope, and, in gaining immunity from trial for the king after his arrest and return to Paris and in securing only suspension of his functions until the Constitution should be completed and accepted by him, they made, if not the most, at least much of an exceedingly bad situation.

Leaders of the constitutional party were no doubt aided in a measure by a somewhat favorable turn in public opinion against lawlessness, violence, and democratic and republican anarchical tendencies. Successful return of the king to Paris resulted in a certain feeling of relief, apparently leading to a widespread enhancement of the instinct of national unity, and suppression of the 17 July Champ de Mars outbreaks and reaction against them went far to complete destruction of the direct effectiveness of incipient republican and democratic strength.

Assembly without King: Initial Decisions

The National Assembly was naturally the scene of much excitement on the morning of 21 June, when flight of the king during the night was announced. The fact is in marked contrast with the official report that the news was received "in deep silence." Almost at once the Assembly decided that the ministers should be summoned before it, the decision being fulfilled without delay; [1] and a decree was adopted stipulating that couriers should be dispatched to all parts of the country, informing the administrative and military authorities of the attitude and action expected of them. Proposals of various sorts were naturally offered in great numbers, and, after more or less discussion, some were accepted and others rejected. Among those rejected was a proposal to confer authority on a small body of five men, which was twice voted down. A suggestion by the Minister of the Interior that two members of the Assembly should be associated with him was also refused. The ministers were readily heard. Naturally, an initial question that was raised had to do with the legal status of decisions by the Assembly. The Minister of Justice, Duport-du-Tertre, recalling that he had been appointed by the king, who had entrusted to him the Seal, announced that he had that morning received a communication from the king which ordered all the ministers to refuse to sign any order not emanating from the king and which forbade him to affix the Seal except when so commanded by the king. The Assembly, after a brief discussion, unanimously adopted the following decree:

[1] Montmorin, Minister of Foreign Affairs, was delayed through public manifestations at his residence.

The National Assembly decrees provisionally, and until otherwise ordered, that decrees rendered by it shall be put into execution by the ministers; commands the Minister of Justice to affix
to them the Seal of the State, without need of sanction or acceptance.

And, after somewhat more extended deliberation, a supplementary provision was voted in the following terms:

The Constituent Assembly orders that decrees rendered or to be
rendered without the sanction of the king by reason of his
absence shall none the less provisionally have force of law
throughout the whole extent of the kingdom.

On 22 June announcement of the arrest of the king was
made in the National Assembly. Within the week decrees
were voted concerning surveillance of the king and the royal
family, concerning arrangements for hearing the king, and
concerning guardianship of the heir to the throne.

Assembly without King: Committee Report

On 13 July, a somewhat dull lawyer of the Left, Muguet,
representative of Franche-Comté, reported to the National
Assembly on behalf of seven committees combined—Diplomatic Affairs, Military Affairs, Constitution, Revision, Criminal Jurisprudence, Reports, and Investigations—concerning
the flight of the king. The first part of the long report consisted of a careful, detailed account of all the facts that had
been established. This was followed by an examination of the
character of monarchical government and of the connection
with it of the principle of the inviolability of the monarch.
The conclusions were that the king had in fact committed no
legally defined offense and that in principle, being inviolable,
he could not in any event be brought to trial. Invoking the
distinction between the irresponsibility of the king and the

responsibility of agents, the committees presented to the
Assembly several draft proposals which would have the effect
of inculpating certain military officers and of liberating two
ladies of the royal household. A vigorous effort was made by
the extreme Left to secure postponement of discussion. They
were faced with the fact that the Moderates from the beginning made effective use of the very doubtful premise that the
king had been abducted, and they somewhat naturally felt
that with the passage of time the flight would clearly appear
as a voluntary act. Postponement, however, was defeated by
vote of the Assembly, and the remainder of that day's sitting
and the sittings of the next two days were devoted to debate
which was concerned primarily with the question of the inviolability of the king.

Assembly without King: Debate on Inviolability

The three-day debate on the inviolability of the king was
characterized by much the same qualities as marked most of
the typical discussions in the National Assembly. There was
the same minimum of substance and the same flair for abstract
logic-chopping.

The extreme wing of the Jacobins launched a bitter attack
on the king, concluding that he should be brought to trial.
Members of the Assembly who espoused the opposite side
followed the line taken by Muguet on behalf of the committees. Several speakers insisted that the king had committed
no recognized offenses, and they followed with the argument that in any case the inviolability of the king precluded
his being tried.

The champion debaters for what was essentially the republican cause emphasized the importance of distinctions in
the matter of inviolability. They undertook to differentiate
what was variously referred to as the constitutional or ad-

ministrative or civil irresponsibility of the king from his personal or criminal responsibility. They readily accepted the principle of ministerial responsibility, but they contended vigorously that it applied only to the governmental, not to the personal, actions of the king. Indeed, Robespierre argued that the very fact that ministers could not be responsible for the personal acts of the king required that the principle that the king could do no wrong should in its application be confined to actions for which the ministers could be held responsible, namely, the administrative actions of the king. Another member [2] painted a lurid picture of the heinous offenses which the king, if personally inviolable, might with impunity commit.

Other arguments were not lacking. Thus, it was asserted by the "advanced" Patriot, Abbé Grégoire, representative of Nancy, that to the question what pre-existing law had been violated by the king it was sufficient to answer the supreme law of public safety. Again, contention was made that invocation of the principle of inviolability was irrelevant in view of the fact that Louis was no longer king, having by his actions automatically abdicated.

Speakers who supported the position of the committees held that the distinctions which their opponents urged were untenable. They insisted that the principle that the person of the king was sacred and inviolable was fundamental.[3] Inviolability, they maintained, was not relative but absolute.

The contention that the only limit to inviolability was abdication was well put by Barnave in an excellent speech, which concluded the debate. The young Grenoble lawyer,

[2] An obscure representative recorded as Putraink.

[3] This familiar proposition had, it will be recalled, been voted without difficulty by the National Assembly in September of 1789. Cf. Ch. IV, p. 96n.

somewhat characteristically ignoring the force of extralegal action, asserted that grounds for abdication should be and could only be determined by law. He insisted that the only law concerning abdication was an article which, voted by the Assembly at the end of March despite bitter opposition from the Right, had been worded as follows: "If the King should leave the realm and if, after invitation through a proclamation by the legislative body, he should not return to France, he would be construed to have abdicated." Like other supporters of the committees, Barnave undertook to demonstrate that this provision had in no wise been violated; [4] and, reiterating what had previously been said by Duport, he related the subject of the debate to the very nature of the Revolution and the state at which it had arrived. Recognition of the inviolability of the king, it was asserted, was of the highest importance as indicating that the Revolution had, instead of making a fresh start, reached a desirable halt, and that the cause of liberty had arrived at a much-needed balance with governmental stability and strength.

The high level reached by certain speeches, above the spirit of faction,[5] made a strong impression upon the National Assembly and ensured the triumph of the position of the committees. Several preliminary provisions suggested by an able member [6] were accepted. They were worded as follows:

1. If the king, after taking his oath to the Constitution, shall withdraw it, he shall be considered to have abdicated. 2. If the king shall put himself at the head of an army in order to employ its force against the nation, or if he shall order his generals to carry out such an undertaking, or finally if he shall not oppose

---

[4] Salles, a doctor representing Nancy, in a careful speech of much merit recognized that the king had violated his "obligation"; but he urged the existence of extenuating circumstances.

[5] Like those of Salles and Barnave.   [6] The same Salles.

an action of this kind carried out in his name, he shall be considered to have abdicated. 3. A king who shall have abdicated or who shall be considered to have done so shall become a private citizen and shall be liable to accusation, through the ordinary forms, for all acts subsequent to his abdication.[7]

The proposals of the committees, involving, it will be recalled, inculpation of certain officers and liberation of two ladies of the royal household, were voted without change.

Assembly without King: Increased Subordination of the Ministers

In connection with the flight of the king and its aftermath, during the period, that is to say, extending from the end of June through the month of July, much practice and precedent accumulated which were calculated to have marked influence on development of the executive-legislative relationship and of attitudes and views in the matter.

With the suspension of the king, the ministers naturally came into greater prominence. On 21 June, not only were they given control of the Seal of the State, but the Assembly decreed that foreign ambassadors were to be notified that their relations should be with the ministers. On the same day, the Minister of Foreign Affairs was added to the Committee on Diplomacy, and a few days later the same minister was, after investigation, absolved of responsibility with respect to the passports employed in connection with the king's flight, the crowd which had been surrounding the minister's residence breaking into applause when announcement of the Assembly's decision was made to it.

There was frequent written communication between the National Assembly and the ministers. On occasion, the ministers were at their request heard in the Assembly, though

[7] See *Moniteur*, 1791, no. 199 (18 July), p. 822.

they were jealously prevented from offering specific measures
to it. The tendency was for the ministers to be overshadowed
by the committees. The ministers were frequently criticized
adversely in the Assembly, and they were more and more
often summoned before it. On such occasions, they regularly
assured the Assembly that they could be fully counted upon.
Indeed, as early as 21 June, the ministers assured the Assembly
of their full co-operation with it. On 31 July the Assembly
voted a decree requiring the ministers to attend its sittings on
alternate days. The text of the decree was in part as follows:

The ministers shall be required from now on to come to sittings at two o'clock on one day out of two with a view to
giving information concerning developments in respect of
measures calculated to ensure defense of the realm and to giving
such explanations as shall be requested of them or as they shall
feel disposed to communicate.

From the point of view of the problem of parliamentary
government, establishment in the summer of 1791 of a relationship between legislature and executive that was closer
than discussions of the doctrine of the separation of powers
had been disposed to allow was doubtless in a sense favorable
to development of the political responsibility of ministers;
and yet, before the parliamentary regime was understood
and practiced, forces were at work, it is interesting to observe, tending to subordinate the executive to the legislature
in a degree inconsistent with the harmony and nice balance
characteristic of the system in its ideal form. In other words,
insofar as continuation of a monarchical regime could be
anticipated, conditions following upon the flight of the king
were in general favorable to parliamentary government; but,
in the wider perspective, they were, by a kind of historical
anticipation, favorable to assembly government.

X

Adoption of the Constitution of 3 September 1791

THE last efforts on the part of members and allies of the Committee on the Constitution to establish institutional arrangements favorable to parliamentary monarchy were made during the month of August of 1791, the period within which the final text of the Constitution was voted by the National Assembly. The leaders of the constitutional party, in the face of continuing difficulties and dangers,[1] possessed the understanding and the courage to choose and to support the provisions which were essential to establishment of a strong and stable government, though they thus put themselves in opposition to previous decisions of the Assembly. These leaders announced more than once that the committee was unanimous.

In the end, hope that the Right might lend aid to establish-

---

[1] Villat (*op. cit.*, p. 118) gives a striking summary of the situation: "La peur des clubs, la rivalité des partis ne vont pas permettre de reviser à fond la Constitution, et les débats de juillet et d'août vont présenter un caractère incohérent et morne qui traduit la lassitude des deputés et la défiance de l'opinion."

ment of a parliamentary monarchy, which was the sole possibility of weakening the coalition of the two wings of the Assembly against the center, turned out to be forlorn. Moreover, the parliamentary situation constituted a limitation upon the opportunity for initiative of the committee. In this respect, the Assembly had, in September of 1790, decreed that there should be

associated with the Committee on the Constitution seven members, elected from the total membership of the Assembly, in order, concurrently with the Committee on the Constitution, to examine all the decrees that have been issued by the National Assembly, to separate out those which form the Constitution proper from those which have the character only of statutes or regulations, to make thus a corpus of constitutional acts, and to verify the formulation of the articles with a view to rectifying errors which might have slipped into them.[2]

The committee understandably felt that it was not empowered to make fundamental textual changes, and its anticipation of bitter opposition was borne out by the fact that it was forced to defend against attack some of its timid proposals, which it conceived it was authorized to make by virtue of the instruction "to separate out."

Final Constitutional Discussion

On 5 August, Thouret, on behalf of the Committees on the Constitution and on Revision, appeared before the National Assembly with the draft text of the Constitution. Observing that there was at the moment no occasion for discussion but commenting on the appropriateness of the anniversary date for his task, he read through the long set of provisions. Three days later, he asked and after brief discussion received approval by the Assembly of the general structure of the

[2] See *Moniteur*, 1790, no. 267 (24 Sept.), p. 1106.

suggested text. Thereupon, consideration *seriatim* of the provisions began.

On about twenty days between 8 August and 3 September, Thouret guided the discussion through its somewhat uneven course. Large numbers of articles were occasionally voted with no discussion. Others were approved with next to none. On the other hand, a provision or a clause or even a word was often the subject of a long, sometimes a bitter, and not infrequently a largely sterile debate. Similarly with respect to alterations, some were accepted without question, others were as cavalierly rejected, while still others were approved or refused only after lengthy discussion. A certain number of provisions were such as to require, before acceptance, further committee consideration and report. Finally, the Assembly was informed on 27 August that it had voted the complete Constitution with the exception of the provisions on the method of amendment. This subject gave rise to considerable delay, occasioned by discussion, altercation, and recommittal; but the provisions were adopted on 3 September, and the Assembly decreed that no further changes would be considered.

On 13 September the Minister of Justice handed to the president of the National Assembly a letter from the king accepting the Constitution, and on the following day the king, appearing in person, confirmed in a gracious speech his approval of the document. The National Assembly held its last sitting on 30 September. The king appeared again and addressed the Assembly. The president of the Assembly made a few concluding remarks, at the end of which he asserted the conviction that the best government for France was one reconciling the royal prerogative and the rights of the people and announced the view that the Assembly had given the state "a Constitution which guarantees equally royalty and national liberty." Upon this declaration, the substance of which was no doubt characterized more by good intent than by accuracy, the Assembly adjourned.

Final Debate on the Status of Ministers

During the course of final consideration of the Constitution, the subject which was most pertinent to the problem of parliamentary government, namely, the position of the ministers, was also the subject which gave rise on the whole to the most extensive controversial discussion. More particularly, the question of exclusion of members of the legislature from the Ministry of the king was debated a last time. This limitation on the appointive power of the king was not the only matter that received vigorous discussion; subjects like suffrage qualifications and freedom of the press were the basis of warm altercation,[3] but the presence of ministers in the legislature was the central topic of concern. The subject became in some sense a symbol of the deep-running issue between limited monarchy and republicanism.[4] In particular, converts like Barnave and Duport, after what is said to be the manner of converts, were strikingly persistent in their identification of hope for the future with a single and simple cause, namely, that of the ministers as intermediaries between king and nation. They were undeterred by the venom of members of the far Left, whose republican bias was likewise not without the flavor of religious fervor.

Debate by the Assembly in August on the constitutional position of the ministers did not wait for consideration in

[3] Other subjects which were debated with more than average interest included the matter of the King's Guard and the question of the status of the royal family.

[4] Cf., in this respect, Madelin, *Les Hommes de la Révolution*, pt. I, p. 107: "L'exclusion paraît bientôt . . . dogme intangible."

regular order of the articles devoted to the executive. The question was interjected, through the initiative of the extreme Left, into the discussion of the legislature. This came about in connection with the matters of eligibility and compatibility, as involved in the qualifications of members of the legislative body. On 13 August the Assembly had been making a good deal of progress in voting in final form various articles which it had previously approved, when an interruption occurred following the reading of the draft text of the article applying to the ministers. The ministers were now explicitly mentioned, the proposed phraseology being in part as follows:

Art. III. All active citizens, whatever may be their property or tax status, shall be entitled to be chosen as representatives of the nation.

Art. IV. Nevertheless, the ministers and such other agents of the executive power as are removable at will shall be obliged to opt. . . .

A less well-known member of the extreme Left, Saint-Martin, representative of Annonay, intervened to insist that this was the point at which should be considered the provision already voted by the Assembly preventing members of the legislature from becoming ministers. He noted that the provision was entirely omitted from the draft Constitution. His intervention struck the spark which set off the debate.

Aside from the arguments which were at this time developed concerning the merits of the question whether ministers should be members of the legislature, two formal contentions were made which, though more relevant in some measure to dilatory motions, were not without pertinence to the problem of parliamentary government. In the first place, Thouret's immediate reply to Saint-Martin was that the question which was raised, and therefore discussion of it, should properly come later, if at all. The implications from the point of view of formal logic were, no doubt, clear enough. Whether or not ministers were eligible to be chosen to the legislature was manifestly a question which was connected with election and hence with the elective branch of government; whether or not a member of the legislature could be chosen to be a minister was a question related to the scope of the appointing power, and hence to the executive branch. As a practical matter, Thouret was perhaps unwise in not recognizing the close interrelationship between the two sides of the question. Consistent application of a doctrine dear to the extreme Left, that of popular sovereignty, might have proved embarrassing to Saint-Martin. If free choice on the part of the people included the right, if desired, to select a minister, the legitimate logical converse would seem to have been that a member of the legislature could be chosen minister on condition that he submit himself to re-election. This prevailing English practice, though it had previously been somewhat vaguely referred to in the Assembly, was not brought into the discussion on the occasion of the final constitutional debate. It was indeed scarcely relevant in view of the stipulation in the pending article that a minister, if elected, must opt between the two positions involved. Even here, logic might have suggested that, if the principle involved in the question of compatibility was that of the separation of powers, the principle would have been satisfied with the arrangement, incorporated in American constitutions [5] and

[5] Restrictions, such as those contained in the Constitution of the United States with respect to newly established positions or positions of which the emoluments may have recently been increased, do not limit in principle, and rarely limit in practice, the appointive power of the executive.

already practised in the National Assembly, whereby members of the legislature could, on condition of the same option, be made ministers. For the extreme Left, the matter had, however, become a symbolic element in a position on which they would not yield.

If Thouret could reasonably argue that the question of appointment of members of the legislature to the Ministry should not have been treated in provisions relating to the legislative branch of the government, he and his friends were, in terms of formal procedure, on decidedly less solid ground in defending omission altogether of stipulations concerning the matter. Whereas opponents of the committees had themselves insisted, in the debate concerning re-eligibility of representatives, on the distinction between a constituent and a legislative body, speakers for the committee position respecting the ministers undertook to distinguish the National Assembly, as a *revolutionary* body, from the legislature which it was, through a written constitution, about to establish. Thus, the previous decision by the Assembly forbidding the appointment of representatives as ministers, which Duport referred to as a generous action on the part of the Assembly, was contended by Thouret to be a revolutionary precaution, not required in the case of a regular legislative assembly. However, the fact that the formal distinction was plausible would scarcely seem to have been sufficient to bring within the terms of reference of the committees omission by them of a question viewed by both sides as so important. Another member of the extreme Left, Prieur, representative of Châlons-sur-Marne, was quick to point out that the Assembly's decision in the matter had been decreed "constitutionally." This he doubtless regarded as sufficient to determine the question on the basis of terms of reference. In any case, he did not, as he might have done, further undermine

Thouret's position by pointing out that the Assembly's decision explicitly mentioned not only its own members but those of future representative bodies as well. Tracy insisted that Prieur's argument was "detestable," estopping any improvement with respect to matters concerning which the Assembly had already pronounced. He gave examples of things that had been decreed "constitutionally" by the Assembly which he asserted with some reason no one would wish to see introduced into the Constitution. He strongly underlined the importance of the conditions in which the Assembly's decision had been taken. These, he asserted, included the facts that it was "decreed without discussion and without examination, formulated in the midst of tumult, and decreed, so to say, without being heard." His insistence that the matter should be argued on its merits was doubtless a sound conclusion, though his argument itself would appear to have confused the power of the Assembly to modify its own decisions and the authority of the committees as defined in their terms of reference. Thouret and the committees had taken the initiative in giving to the discussion its oblique direction; and, though Thouret might, like any other member, have suggested modification of the Assembly's decision, he undertook on behalf of the committees a maneuver which consisted in attempting, through a formal distinction, to support a position which consisted in reality of an argument on the merits.

So far as arguments on the merits were concerned, Thouret and his friends, though they were from the nature of the case unable to advance anything essentially new, made a strong case along accepted lines. They contended vigorously that a rigid separation of powers gave rise to hostility between the legislature and executive, whereas what was needed was harmony. In the latter respect, only co-operation, they felt, would result in the energy that was requisite for effective government. To these considerations Duport added one that he clearly thought was calculated to appeal to his former Jacobin friends, namely, the desirability of a popular basis for the executive. Given the system that was contemplated, no other way was possible, he argued, to bring the executive into relationship with the people except to take the ministers from among the representatives of the nation.

Opponents, in turn, rang the changes on the danger of corruption. Thus the eloquent jurist, Roederer, representative of Metz, starting with an assertion of the importance of respect by the people for the laws, argued that such an attitude could exist only where the people possessed an almost religious belief not merely that corruption was absent from lawmaking but that there was no possibility that it could be present.

Thouret countered with a contention which he had made before, that corruption would not result from any particular relationship of executive and legislature, but was a risk, insofar as risk was involved, inherent in the very nature of representative government. He suggested with no little insight that the most important guarantee against corruption would exist where ministers, being taken from and present in the legislature, championed a policy which was supported by a majority and opposed by a minority ready to furnish other ministers when their policy should receive the support of a majority. This plea for an arrangement which would favor development of an organized opposition was somewhat strangely misapprehended by Roederer. Himself confused, he professed to find complete confusion in the position of Thouret, who underlined the importance of harmony between legislature and executive only to advocate an organized opposition.

The debate on 13 August represented the last occasion on which the issue was joined in the National Assembly concerning the taking of ministers from among the representatives of the people. Whatever the merits of the arguments, the committees and their supporters were bested by the champions of the separation of powers. Closure of the debate was voted by the Assembly, following demands from all parts of the house. Just previous to the final vote, Buzot succeeded in securing acceptance of an amendment reducing from four years to two the period during which, following a term, members of a legislature remained precluded from appointment to the executive. The official report of the Assembly's action was worded as follows:

The Assembly adopted the proposal by M. Buzot, and decrees that the members of the present Assembly and those of subsequent legislatures may not be chosen to any place given by the executive power until two years after the end of their session.

On the following day, 14 August, the Assembly voted without discussion the six articles presented under the rubric *Ministers*, namely, those stipulating for the king's power of appointment and removal, for countersignature, for legal responsibility, for financial accountability, and so on.[6] In the final text of the Constitution, the decree of 13 August

[6] In the *Arch. parl.* (XXIX [14 Aug. 1791], 434), an incident is reported concerning which the *Moniteur* is silent. Saint-Martin is represented as asking what had become of the decree of 6 April stating that the legislature might declare that the Ministry had not its confidence. Thouret is made to reply that in the opinion of the committees the provision had no place in a constitution; the king might ignore the declaration.

forbidding choice of members of the legislature as ministers was, in perfected form, inserted after the first of the articles concerned with the ministers.

The defeat suffered by the committees and their supporters when the Assembly voted the decree of 13 August was undoubtedly a crucial one. Their opponents became more fully aware of an increased strength; they themselves learned how slight were their chances of salvaging, in the course of the adoption of the Constitution, anything of much substance for the cause of parliamentary monarchy and stable government.

The fact that both sides had come to regard the matter of ministers from and in the legislature as the capital constitutional issue, reflecting the deep-running cleavage in public opinion, was demonstrated by the tenseness and bitterness which, on occasion of the vote of the decree, prevailed among members of the Assembly and among the spectators. An apparently chance word of a speaker set off a disorderly hubbub. Barnave finally was given the floor; and, quickly transcending and causing to be forgotten the incident which had given rise to the violent scene, he pronounced an able but disillusioned and bitter speech, directed in large part straight at the more scurrilous members of the extreme Left. In respect of the Constitutional situation, the speech was primarily a *post mortem*. Barnave referred to the hopes and the disappointments of the committees, to their own doubt even before the debate whether they ought not to resign. He set out clearly the general character of the terms of reference, the great complexity of the provisions with which the committees had been constrained to deal, and the basic aims of the committees in formulating a consistent text, namely, to combine in a nice balance liberty with stability and durability. "You have," he declared, "already cut from our work modifications we had judged indispensable to the effective success of the Constitution." He could conclude only by urging the Assembly to be careful about its future actions and by pleading for a better spirit in its work.

On the following day, 14 August, Thouret, before setting out in his methodical way to secure adoption of various sections of draft articles, asked the indulgence of the Assembly for a general statement on behalf of the committees. His *post mortem* was somewhat more precise than that of Barnave. He said:

We took all possible precautions against the danger of too great prerogatives that might have been accorded to the executive power. We calculated scrupulously all that could be cut from its power without taking away the force necessary to government, and we allowed to remain only what, in our opinion, was absolutely necessary. Everything in our plan was necessary, coherent, and perfectly connected. Every change was obliged to alter it. It was in replacing the former powerful means of the executive power with facility and latitude for the king confidently to choose his agents that we have thought that with a king attached to the Constitution we might have a good government.

His conclusion was for the sake, so to say, of the record:

Your committees have therefore taken into consideration the results of the changes beginning yesterday effected in our plan through the deliberations of the Assembly, and we have recognized unanimously that the limitations put upon elections, along with prohibition placed on the king to take from expiring legislatures the agents necessary to him, destroyed all the means of force and energy for the executive power. Our unanimity on so delicate a matter has led us to think that we ought to make a last declaration concerning the unaltered opinion of the committees, not that we wished to make formal proposals on

this subject, but because at the moment that we draw near to
a responsibility which though common is especially applicable
to committees which have done the preparatory work for the
Assembly, we thought that it was important for each of the
members of the Assembly to meditate again upon these questions before the Constitutional Act is completed.[7]

Seats for Ministers on the Floor of the Legislature

Although the text of the Constitution which Thouret had
read to the National Assembly on 5 August omitted provisions several times approved by the Assembly prohibit-
ing the king from choosing ministers from among the
representatives of the people, the draft did contain an article
recognizing an arrangement which had become established
in practice by the Assembly, namely, the admission of ministers to the floor of the legislative body. This omission and
this stipulation appear clearly to have represented a moderate form of the hopes of the leaders of the constitutional
party with respect to what might be salvaged for the benefit
of a strong and stable executive. Their hand had been forced
by their opponents when fact of the omission was brought
to the attention of the Assembly and that body was prevailed
upon to reaffirm its decision against membership of ministers
in the legislature.

The constitutional leaders, in spite of their defeat, proceeded with their plan. In somewhat altered form, the proposal of the committees was adopted by the Assembly. Thus,
the Constitution of 1791 was to contain a stipulation on the
incompatibility of the positions of minister and representative, together with a provision granting seats to ministers in
the legislature, a combination which the experience of coun-

[7] The record notes that Thouret's conclusion gave rise to "de
violens murmures dans l'extrémité gauche."

tries like Norway and the Netherlands has shown not to prevent in itself the effective operation of the parliamentary system. Moreover, the fact that numberless later constitutions of France and of other European countries, though eliminating the stipulation concerning incompatibility, have at the same time retained arrangements for the free entrance of ministers—and even civil servants—to the floor has given rise to a combination which, it may be suggested, is even more convenient in practice, especially for bicameral legislatures, than is the traditional British institution.

The draft text of the article concerning entrance of ministers to the floor of the legislative body, brought by Thouret before the National Assembly on 15 August, was worded as follows:

The ministers of the king shall have entrance to the National Legislative Assembly; they shall have a marked place in it; they shall be heard on all matters concerning which they shall so request, and every time that they shall be required to give clarifications.

The doctrinaires returned to the attack, led by Robespierre. The Incorruptible asserted that the proposal "perverted the principal article of the Constitution," violated, in other words, the doctrine of the separation of powers. He insisted with some plausibility that under the arrangement which was suggested ministers would differ from representatives only in having no vote. He contended, likewise reasonably enough, that ministers would regard this difference as of little importance. Their real aim, he argued with perhaps less reason in view of the overtones resulting from the frequent warnings against corruption, would be to "influence the deliberations"; for they would be, he insisted in elaborating his point, "clothed with the right to direct the delibera-

tions and to exercise a direct influence on the formation of
the law." In this respect, the dogmatic character of a dialectic
which avoided examination on its merits of executive leadership by assuming its viciousness as contrary to the largely
undefined premise of the separation of powers was demonstrated by other extremist Jacobins. Thus, at one point, the
Alsatian extreme Leftist, Rewbel, exclaimed: "Speak French!
Say that you want them to have the initiative"; and Pétion,
another ally of Robespierre, insisted that it would have been
more consistent to propose that "the making of the law in
its entirety be abandoned" to the ministers.

On the side of the committee article, several speakers displayed evidence of some insight into the principles of parliamentary government. Even Barère, who insisted that the
draft article went too far, appeared unwilling to deny the
accumulated experience of the National Assembly. As he
said:

No doubt it is wise to admit the ministers to a place in the
Assembly and to authorize them when required to do so to give
clarifications; no doubt it is useful that when conferences with
the minister are necessary they be held in full Assembly and
not in the secrecy of committees.

Beaumetz, in arguing in more moderate vein that the presence
of ministers on the floor of the legislature, where they could
point out defects in pending legislation, would render less
likely employment of the veto, appeared to sense instinctively
the vigorous working of the logic of things which has caused
withholding of the royal assent to legislation to fall into
desuetude in Great Britain. And Barnave, ignoring like other
members involved the taunting accusations by former Jacobin
colleagues of arguing inconsistently with their position at
the time of the defeat of Mirabeau on the same principle,

closed the debate in his habitually clear manner. Of the ministers he said:

It is indispensable that they be habitually in the Assembly, whether to give answer to divers interpellations or to share with it their knowledge. It is through the absence of ministers that vague denunciations have taken shape in public opinion, and it is in the same way that a minister of bad faith can elude a well-founded accusation. They must be taken and told: "Why did you do that? Why did you not do that?"

A man of good faith, he continued, would want to be questioned openly about everything. Barnave repeated succinctly Beaumetz' argument about the veto; and, with respect to the repeated arguments concerning corruption and to the frequent reference to England, he contented himself with saying that opponents showed profound ignorance of conditions in Britain in not knowing that members were not corrupted by ministers in Parliament but were corrupted before entering.

During the debate on the entrance of ministers to the floor of the legislative body, several speakers found fault with the working of the committee proposal rather than with its essential idea. At the end of the concluding speech by Barnave, Charles de Lameth, undertaking to reconcile the views that had been expressed, suggested a draft that was voted by the Assembly and subsequently incorporated, with the change of only a word or two, into the Constitution of 1791. The article, as proposed by De Lameth, was worded as follows:

The ministers of the king shall have entrance to the legislative assembly; they shall have a marked place; they shall be heard every time they shall request it on matters relative to their administration, or when they shall be required to give clarifications. They shall likewise be heard on matters foreign to their administration every time that the legislative body shall grant them the floor.

The Ministers and the Initiative in Finance

Toward the end of the discussion of the Constitution, when the Assembly on 26 and 27 August was dealing with some miscellaneous provisions that had been passed over, the position of ministers came in for final notice in connection with a special topic. The draft text of the Constitution that had been read to the Assembly on 5 August included, among the provisions relating to the royal sanction, an article forbidding the tacking of riders to fiscal measures and an article listing some eight or ten subjects respecting which decisions by the legislative body would not require the royal sanction. Fiscal matters did not form one of these subjects. On 26 August, Desmeuniers, on behalf of the Committees on the Constitution and on Revision, read to the Assembly a draft text which proposed to exempt fiscal measures from the need of royal sanction and which incorporated with this suggestion the previous proposal concerning riders.

A first speaker, Pison, another lawyer of Dauphiné, asserted briefly, no reason being given, that fiscal measures ought not to be exempt from the royal sanction but that appropriation measures ought. The next two speakers, Beaumetz and Duport, argued that the important thing was to give the initiative in public finance to the ministers. The first, offering a proposal which he requested to be sent to the committee, based his contention on the need for continuity; the second urged the lack of responsibility of legislatures in the matter of finance.

The sitting here came to an end; and, on the following day, Beaumetz reported that the Committees on the Consti-

tution and on Revision had met jointly with the Committee
on Fiscal Affairs, with the result that they suggested, almost
unanimously, leaving the original proposal intact and adding
a further provision. This addition proposed "to require the
ministers to give their opinion concerning the means of an-
nually providing the funds necessary to meet the expenditures of the State." After a member had suggested that the
provision was useless in view of the arrangement for affording entrance of the ministers to the legislature, Barère made
a speech that was exceedingly long, frequently applauded,
somewhat pompous, and scarcely indicative of much insight.
At what seemed unnecessary length, he labored the fundamental importance of ultimate legislative power of the purse.
From this he deduced, in view of his allegation that "the
executive power will always be the enemy of the legislative
power," the proposition that any initiative on the part of
the ministers in respect of finance would be fraught with the
most serious danger. Indeed, he proclaimed that if he wished
to re-establish the Old Regime at its worst, he could not conceive of a better means to the end. The discussion being
closed with some impatience on the part of the Assembly, the
additional provision was rejected; and the original proposal
was voted without further discussion.

The Constitution and National Sovereignty

In the course of the discussion of the Constitution that
took place in the National Assembly between 5 August and
3 September, a few events occurred which, without being
directly connected with the position of the ministers, were
relevant to the problem of parliamentary government. Thus,
the stipulation denying to the king the power of dissolution
of the legislative body was voted on 10 August; articles
concerning the inviolability of the king and concerning his

abdication were approved on 13 August; and provisions concerning the royal sanction were accepted on 15 August. The draft text in these several respects was incorporated at various points in the committee proposals, and this text was, along with numerous related articles, voted with little or no discussion. The only further extended discussion worthy of note took place early in the period of final passage of the Constitution, namely, on 10 August. The subject, being markedly abstract, gave rise to some characteristically doctrinaire speeches.

On 10 August the National Assembly had arrived at Title III of the draft Constitution. As reporter Thouret could have congratulated himself that things were going relatively well. He had with little mishap steered the discussion through the Declaration of Rights and its Preamble and through Titles I and II, concerned respectively with certain fundamental constitutional guarantees and with the territorial structure of the country and the status of citizens. Title III, dealing with the public powers, was of course the heart of the Constitution. It was the only title to be subdivided into chapters and sections as well as articles, this arrangement being unchanged in the completed Constitution. Placed before the several chapters of Title III were five prefatory articles, here again the form and substance of the committee proposals being incorporated into the Constitution as finally accepted. Concerning the first two of these preliminary articles considerable discussion arose.

The text of Article II of Title III, as proposed by the Committees and as incorporated in the Constitution, was worded as follows: "The Nation, from which alone emanate all powers, can exercise them only through delegation.—The French Constitution shall be representative: the representatives shall be the Legislative Body and the King."

The jurist Roederer initiated debate through taking exception to the idea that the king was a representative of the
nation. He sustained this objection in a long and closely
reasoned, if not highly persuasive, speech.[8] Having insisted
that the only correct definition of a representative could
envisage nothing except a person who was popularly elected,
his negative conclusion with respect to the king naturally
followed. Roederer was thus employing abstract concepts
to urge that subordination of the executive to the legislature
be accepted as part of a credo.

This was a striking early example of the phenomenon that
has retained all its vitality down to the present day. In 1791
it was the more interesting as being carefully expressed with
the more mystical overtones of the concept of national sovereignty. "The essence of representation," asserted Roederer,
"is that each individual who is represented lives and deliber-
ates in his representative and that he has by free choice fused
his will in its."

Robespierre followed on the same plane. He had already
thrown striking light on the overtones of national sovereignty
and assembly government through an intervention in the
debate in May of 1790 on the power of war and peace. He
gave rise to disorder and to demands from the Right that he
be called to order when he said: "It is not right to speak of
representative of the Nation. The king is the *commis* and
the delegate of the nation to carry out the national will." [9]

---

[8] "Froidement élégant" is the appraisal by Duvergier de Hauranne,
op. cit., I, 203, 205, of this speech by Roederer "que l'on avait vu
successivement quitter les Jacobins pour le club de 1789, le club de
1789 pour les Jacobins, les Jacobins pour les Feuillants, et les Feuillants pour les Jacobins."

[9] *Moniteur*, 1790, no. 139 (19 May), p. 561. The word *commis*, to
which exception was so strongly taken by the Right, is a difficult
one for which to find a suitable English translation. At present, it is

In the final debate on the Constitution, Robespierre wished to go beyond Roederer's reasoning. While agreeing with the jurist that the king was not a representative of the nation, he was especially opposed to the general proposition that *powers* could be delegated. This, he insisted, was inconsistent with the *inalienability of sovereignty*, a concept proclaimed in the immediately preceding article. Invoking, as often appeared his great pleasure, the pronouncements of Rousseau, he repeated his familiar insistence on the importance of distinguishing powers and functions. His conclusion was that only the legislature possessed powers, and that it could consequently delegate to the executive, which could in turn possess, only functions. Other speakers followed along similar lines.

On the other side, speakers in favor of the text of the committee joined square issue on the nature of representation. Employing a definition of representative that underlined function rather than source, members such as Thouret and Barnave contended strongly for a concept that would legitimately include the king. Barnave was particularly effective, showing himself easily capable of replying on an abstract and mystical level. "What distinguishes," he asserted, "the representative from the public functionary is that the representative can will for the nation, whereas the public functionary can only act for it." On this basis, he felt there was no difficulty in showing that the king was to be placed

---

a word persistently employed with respect to the ministers by those who criticize the French parliamentary system as being one of assembly government. As for the situation in the early Revolution, Chevallier, *Histoire des institutions politiques*, p. 37, says simply: "Les ministres sont traités en commis"; and Villat, *op. cit.*, p. 94, gives the same picture, *comités* communicating directly with agents of administration and the ministers being treated "comme de simples commis."

in the first category, not in the second as the doctrinaire speakers had insisted.

In the result, the proposal with which Roederer had concluded his intervention, involving several substantial alterations of the committee text, was rejected. On the other hand, Thouret had as reporter readily accepted certain amendments which had been proposed during the discussion with respect to the first article. This had originally proclaimed that "sovereignty is one, indivisible and belongs to the nation; no section of the people can arrogate to itself exercise of it." The accepted amendments, which were incorporated into the completed text of the Constitution, added the epithets *inalienable* and *imprescriptible* to the description of sovereignty; and every *individual,* as well as section of the people, was estopped from appropriating the exercise of sovereignty.

The minor success of the committees and of the constitutional party in resisting terminology which would plainly have stated that the king and the executive possessed a distinctly subordinate position would appear to have been of little lasting consequence in France. The king has disappeared; and, in a parliamentary republic, a subordinate position for the executive has become a widely advocated concept, continually manifesting itself in varying but always considerable measure in practice. The definitive success of far-reaching change along lines that General de Gaulle has followed to strengthen the executive in France is, of course, possible; but belief in such a possibility may well be seriously to underestimate the persistence and permanence of the tradition of the Revolution.

Conclusion

RETROSPECTIVE reflection concerning the constitutional activity of the National Assembly of 1789–1791 would seem to find its most natural initial point in the simple consideration that the final product of the Assembly's work was strikingly short-lived. At the same time, the question whether the excellence of a governmental system is properly to be measured by its actual ability to survive is far from a simple one. There can be little if any doubt that a constitution which might be accepted as in some sense the best in the world could be conceived as succumbing to irresistible forces. On the other hand, the failure of a constitution in a given case might, it seems reasonable to suppose, be interconnected with such a complexus of problems that confident conclusions, in the absence of acceptance of a specific philosophy of history and of agreement on the precise weight to be accorded to the various related events, are scarcely to be anticipated.

The Constitution of 3 September 1791, viewed from this distance, can hardly be regarded as in any ordinary sense a good constitution. That, in other circumstances, it might conceivably have survived for a respectable period may be admitted without necessary implication that the hypothesis is of any marked importance for constitutional history. To set out an account of the conditions in which the political system that resulted from the work of the Assembly of 1789–1791 manifested its defects in practice would be to extend the account of a period beyond the period and to rewrite the history of another period. There would still remain the problem of the reciprocal influence of system and events. Answer to the question what part was played by the defects of the regime would seem clearly to imply prior consideration of those defects. This would certainly appear to be a task for analysis.

Appraisal of the principal characteristics of the Constitution that was formulated by the National Assembly and judgment of the political system that the Constitution envisaged would do well to distinguish certain fundamental principles from important institutional arrangements. The two are no doubt reciprocally connected, but the principles, as the consciously intended bases for the institutions, can claim a natural priority. A first concluding word ought to be said about the principle of the separation of powers and the concept of national sovereignty.

The Separation of Powers

The great reverence which large numbers of members of the National Assembly of 1789–1791 had for the doctrine of the separation of powers is a most striking phenomenon. This kind of regard was indubitably unfavorable to the development of the parliamentary system of government.

In the retrospect of experience, the doctrine of the separation of powers may be seen to involve certain considerations that are calculated to cause some wonder at its influence. Probably no two modern scholars who have concerned themselves seriously with the doctrine are in agreement.

Differences about whether powers actually exist to be separated, how many there are if they may be assumed to exist, and so on, hardly leave the impression of a very specific doctrine; and differences of application, observable for example in the fact that the doctrine is invoked in the homeland of Montesquieu to justify the existence of two sets of courts whereas in the United States it serves as a basis for an executive-legislative relationship that is nonparliamentary, tends to confirm such negative impression.

In point of fact, approval of the American form of application of the principle of the separation of powers was widely prevalent in France in the Assembly of 1789–1791. Strong insistence on the rightness of maintaining as great a separation as possible between the executive and legislative branches of government, buttressed with such a view as that of the eternal enmity of the executive and legislature, could hardly be expected to result in much sympathy for the ideal of harmony which is that of the parliamentary system.

National Sovereignty

The key position that has been occupied by the abstract concept of *sovereignty* throughout the history of political thought scarcely needs underlining. As a result of discussions of the concept at various times in various places, the concept has inevitably become overlaid with diverse and complex connotations. In France, association of the concept with the king had, before 1789, a history of much interest and importance. The work of the Revolution in transferring sovereignty in theory and in fact from the king to the nation, between whom there had hitherto been conceived to exist a "mystical marriage," meant not only that concepts associated previously with the king became associated in the minds of the Revolutionary leaders with the nation but also that the mystical character of many of the qualities involved were enhanced in the process of transference from a single concrete individual to an abstract multiform entity.

Insistence on a careful distinction between the *possession* of authority and its *exercise* has undoubtedly been a highly important French contribution to clarity of thought. In the case of an individual, he may manifestly be conceived to *possess* authority in a given case regardless of whether he *exercises* it himself, through another, or not at all. On the other hand, when authority is conceived to be *possessed* by a corporate entity, such authority clearly can be exercised in practice only by one or more individuals; and if the corporate entity is conceived to be characterized by certain mystical moral qualities, possession is likely to be so emotionally stressed that practical problems and actual relations in the matter of exercise will greatly risk being viewed and treated in a confused manner. However all that may be, the awesome regard which many members of the Assembly of 1789–1791 had for national sovereignty indubitably constituted a condition unfavorable for the development of the parliamentary system of government.

Belief in a definite transference of supreme power from king to nation was, it is clear, scarcely conducive to acceptance of the desirability of reconciling the traditional position of the one with the legitimate aspirations of the other. The fact that the king was strongly held to derive his position from the nation had as an inevitable consequence insistence that this position was one of subordination. This, in turn, could hardly be viewed as consistent with the ideal of a nice balance, which is characteristic of the parliamentary system. The very awe in which the concept of national sovereignty was held and the very rigor with which it was advocated made for a rigid intransigence that offered little fertile ground for the gradual development which was required in order for reconciliation to become a practical solution.

Importance of the concept of national sovereignty in the history of parliamentary government in France is by no means to be measured merely by the part it played in preventing the system from being established by the National Assembly of 1789–1791. Influence of the concept has prevailed throughout that history. More particularly, the influence was a highly important factor in development of what came to be in the Third Republic the characteristic form of the French parliamentary system. Nothing that has happened since, not even establishment of the Fifth Republic, can be said basically to alter the fact that this traditional form is indigenous to France, adapted in spite of everything to French needs and to French temperament.

The Alsatian scholar, Professor Robert Redslob, has characterized the French parliamentary system of the Third Republic as an "inauthentic" variant of the "genuine" English system.[1] This striking difference, which has been phrased in various ways, is recognized by Redslob, as it would be certain to be recognized in any serious study, to involve causes of much complexity. At the same time, Redslob attaches no little importance to the fact that parliamentary government has been combined with republicanism in modern France. This view doubtless rests on some foundation, but conclusion in the matter is exceedingly uncertain. The distinction between monarchy and republic involves, as is well known, no necessary difference other than that of the title of the head of state. Differences of overtone, of traditional sentimental associations, exist, it is true, varying with time and place; but such differences, while real enough, are so intangible as largely to defy definite formulation.

[1] *Op. cit.*, pp. 156 ff.

The parliamentary system of the Third Republic was of course classified by Redslob as "inauthentic" because of the comparative weakness of the executive branch of government. Yet this weakness clearly did not prevent the regime from being relatively long-lived. The view may well be correct which attributes to absence of a democratic basis the shorter life of the French parliamentary system that followed upon the Restoration, and yet manifestly the greater stability of a democratically based system like that of the Third Republic would scarcely have suffered, to say the least, from the existence of a relatively strong executive. On the other hand, to say that French parliamentary monarchy with a democratic basis after the Restoration or parliamentary government with a strong executive, whether monarchical or republican, after 1875 would have survived as a "genuine" system is so hypothetical as to be not very meaningful. Each part of the hypothesis involves a supposition contrary to fact. The cause or causes in such matters transcend formal institutional arrangements; and, even if such arrangements ought not to be ignored, a consideration like national character is clearly more fundamental.

How the French executive may be permanently strengthened through any expedient more specific than that of modification of national temperament is probably an insoluble question. Certainly, to propose monarchy as a possible solution at the present day seems unreal. Thus, the basic republicanism of France had become so strongly established that it was difficult to understand why Winston Churchill should have hinted during the Second World War at approval of French monarchical restoration. Even if the problem of succession to De Gaulle should be regarded as making such restoration more attractive, or even relatively more likely, it would be a bold prophet who would confidently anticipate this eventuality. Whether there is some definite sense in which the position of the formal head of state determines the strength of the real executive is, tenable or not, largely an irrelevant question if the position that is proposed is highly unlikely. This is to repeat the doubt whether any important permanent alteration is possible in the absence of change in national character.

Membership of the Executive in the Legislature

With the advantage of hindsight based on some acquaintance with the history and nature of parliamentary government, little if any difficulty attaches to comprehending how the doctrine of the separation of powers and the principle of national sovereignty are fundamentally inconsistent with most of the characteristic features of the system. Study of the activities of the National Assembly in France during the first two years of the Revolution has as an advantage that it throws considerable light on the practical effects of such inconsistency.

There would seem to be unanimous agreement on the part of English constitutional historians that the parliamentary system as it has come to be known could not have been developed in Britain if the provision of the Act of Settlement which would have had the effect of forbidding Ministers of the Crown to serve as members of the House of Commons had been maintained. In view of the fact that the provision was repealed before going into operation and that membership of ministers in the House of Commons became a central feature of the cabinet system, an attempt to disprove the proposition that the system could not have developed without the feature would be highly academic. The successful operation of parliamentary government in places like Norway and the Netherlands, whatever may turn out to be the case in the Fifth Republic in France, suggests avoidance of too forthright a dogmatism in the matter; but these examples would seem to be essentially effects rather than causes in the process of history.

The importance of the fact that membership of ministers in the legislature came to be increasingly unacceptable to a majority of the Assembly of 1789–1791 can scarcely be exaggerated. It was a striking consequence that the body which at one time enthusiastically approved the king for selecting ministers from the Assembly ended by establishing a constitutional limitation markedly more stringent than that which had recently been established in the Constitution of the United States. Although the doctrine of the separation of powers was invoked both in America and in France, the climate of opinion among the constitution makers in the home of Montesquieu was, it can hardly be denied, characterized by a considerably greater degree of distrust and of rigid doctrinaire intransigence.

Perhaps we of the twentieth century, for whom any conflict between a separation of powers and membership of executive leaders in the legislature is largely a formal one, are, as the late G. K. Chesterton suggested, incapable of understanding the depth of feeling in eighteenth-century France concerning the doctrine of the separation of powers. If Chesterton was right, we are doubtless still more incapable of comprehending how greatly this feeling was transcended by regard for the principle of national sovereignty. It seems that certain moderate defenders of monarchy in the National Assembly instinctively felt that a mystical and awesome belief in the absolute supremacy of the nation would, by a certain relentless logic, lead inevitably to advocacy of republicanism. This is an important reason why membership of ministers in the legislature came to be a central issue in the eyes of these moderate members, who regarded this institution as essential for the survival of monarchy. The more extremist champions of separation of powers and national sovereignty, accepting with relish the issue and the interpretation, were vigorously hostile to the institution.

Responsibility and Control: Legal and Political

Political responsibility and accountability (as distinguished from legal responsibility and accountability), which are characteristic of parliamentary government, were clearly not altogether beyond the understanding of certain members of the Assembly of 1789–1791. At the same time, for a majority the somewhat subtle distinction was, if not incomprehensible, at least uncongenial.

A legislature which through mistrust remains separate from the executive will insist on a clearly defined relationship to it. A legislature which represents the supremacy of the nation will undertake to maintain that this relationship is one of superiority to the executive. In this context, the relationship will be defined by law and will operate through it. Responsibility and accountability, if legal in character, will operate only where actions contrary to law are involved. If the question is envisaged at all whether responsibility and accountability can be very effective after the fact, the answer is likely to be, especially on the part of those whose flair for abstraction leads them to emphasize the operation of law rather than the men who operate it, that such is the nature of law. The greater practical efficacy of a responsibility and an accountability that may operate before the law can be broken is an idea too subtle or too paradoxical for champions of the rigidly logical and formally legal. All this was strikingly illustrated in the National Assembly in the famous controversy concerning the veto.

Royal Sanction for Legislation

As is well known, the relentless working of the logic of events has in Great Britain transcended the operation of legal provision in causing to fall into desuetude royal refusal to assent to legislation. This development—which after all had in 1789 run only one-third of its course as now known—was undoubtedly clear to some members of the National Assembly, through their understanding both of principle and of British practice.

Here again, however, the principle of national sovereignty and the doctrine of the separation of powers worked against maintenance of a royal prerogative that, abstractly viewed, seemed manifestly the power of an absolute monarch. What a majority of the members of the Assembly seemed unable to understand, especially in the prevailing conditions of over-heated popular sentiment, was that, according to a simple paradox, limitation of royal power would actually increase it. Members who understood the nature of limited monarchy, though their influence was inevitably weakened by uncongenial momentary partnership in the matter with champions of the Old Regime, had no real fear of theoretical power which they knew would be modified in practice to the point of not being employed; whereas they understood what the majority did not, that a "suspensive veto" by its very establishment involved assumption that it would be used.

Bicameralism and Parliamentary Government

The relationship of bicameralism to the parliamentary system of government is in more than one respect similar to the relationship between that system and the veto. Bicameralism and the veto, unlike political responsibility and the presence of the policy-forming executive in the legislature, are not essential to either the theory or the practice of parliamentary government. On the other hand, the fact that they prevail and for centuries have prevailed in Great Britain causes their association with the parliamentary system to appear a natural one.

Association of bicameralism and the veto with the parliamentary regime undoubtedly seemed natural to the moderate members—Anglophiles—of the National Assembly of 1789–1791. On the other hand, little difficulty should attend understanding that such dual structure was scorned by the extremist advocates of a national sovereignty that was ultimately asserted in the Constitution of 1791 to be *one and indivisible*. Even so, the bitterness of the controversy that arose concerning the two institutions is not altogether easy to comprehend at the present day.

The fact is perhaps noteworthy that the two French Constituent Assemblies of 1945–1946 made bicameralism and the position of the formal head of state into sharply drawn issues. The explanation is to be found, it would seem, not in any necessary theoretical connection of the issues with parliamentary government, but rather in such considerations as the influence of Revolutionary tradition and the practical difficulty of making into real issues differences in degree of emphasis in the matter of approximation to the "genuine" or "authentic" or "classical" variant of the parliamentary system.

Parliamentary Government and Dissolution

If, from an institutional point of view, parliamentary government, whether in its "genuine" or its "inauthentic" form, cannot in principle be conceived to be possible in the absence of close relationship between executive and legislative or in the absence of political responsibility of the execu-

tive to the legislature, whereas it can in principle be conceived
to be possible without the veto or without bicameralism, the
connection between the parliamentary system and the institution of dissolution of the legislature by the executive would
appear to stand somewhere between the two situations. The
proposition would seem at least tentatively acceptable that
parliamentary government in its "classic" form is difficult
to imagine in the absence of a clear-cut and effective operation, actual or potential, of dissolution; whereas the system
in an "inauthentic" form can prevail in practice where arrangement for dissolution exists in a defective form or does
not exist at all.

The view has many times been expressed that the most
important single reform that could be realized in France
would be establishment of an effective arrangement for dissolution, but the problem is by no means without both theoretical and practical difficulty. For example, the experience
of the Weimar Republic, as well as reason and other experience, suggests that, where proportional representation is
employed, the centripetal potentiality of dissolution is largely
offset. Nevertheless, there can, in general, be little doubt
that dissolution is, where it exists, an important element of
strength for the executive which aids it in maintaining a
position of equilibrium, as contrasted with subordination;
but where, as in France, a strong traditional sentiment of
distrust of executive strength prevails, the consideration is
particularly important that sentiment affects institutions at
least as much as it is affected by them.

The institution of dissolution may be regarded as being
highly democratic in character, affording as it does final
word to the people. Indeed, there is in France apparently
unanimous agreement on the point among writers on constitutional matters, in whose works may be found as lucid

analysis of the question as could be desired; and yet a large part of public sentiment has always appeared, in any case before the Fifth Republic, instinctively to conclude that the institution is inconsistent with the principle of national sovereignty. A nation that is conceived to possess mystical qualities presumably projects somehow its soul into a National Assembly, which is the "nation assembled" or the "nation represented"; and though such assembly can of course not be permanent, its revitalizing contact with the nation itself is apparently in some way felt to require solemn renewal at regular periods determined by the nation, not at times agreeable to the pleasure of the executive. Concepts like these, however difficult for persons who are not French fully to understand, were beyond any doubt strongly influential with a majority of the Assembly of 1789–1791.

France and Assembly Government

The various views which in combination determined most of the principal decisions of the National Assembly of 1789–1791, and which, being fundamentally democratic in aspiration, were, though most often not so acknowledged, logically republican in character, were of course to reach their fateful conclusion under the Convention. Accordingly, the *régime conventionnel* has continued to be in a real sense the ideal for which tender regard has always been had by those elements of the French Left that consider themselves to be in the true tradition of the Revolution. Accepting implicitly for the most part the impossibility of literally establishing the system in its original form, these elements retain it as an ideal in the sense that it in large measure determines their aims and that it in practice results in various approximations.

At the present day, to enumerate in order such characteristics as acceptance of a mystical concept of nation and national sovereignty, subordination of the executive to the legislature, elevation of committees to a position of paramount importance, hostility to the institution of dissolution, and so on, is merely to describe the parliamentary system in an "inauthentic" form, the French variant, that is, of parliamentary government. Origins are to be sought in the National Assembly of 1789–1791. All the germs were there. No doubt the origins of parliamentary government and the origins of "inauthentic" characteristics appeared separately, so to say; but this is only to assert that a system which appeared, at least until the time of the Fifth Republic, to have become indigenous had, like all analogous phenomena, to undergo an evolutionary development.

Bibliographical Note

A POLITICAL scientist who undertakes to concern himself with the French Revolution, even though he confines his study to a particular aspect of constitutional history during only two years, is no doubt guilty of considerable temerity. He would add to this no little presumption if he should attempt an elaborate bibliography. He—and the same would be true of any other political scientist who might be tempted to essay a similar study —has the inestimable benefit of the enormous wealth of bibliographical material due to the scholarly work of eminent historians.

In the present study, primary use in the matter of documentary material was of course made of the *Moniteur*, in which the Introduction, Tables, "Analyse," and first 275 numbers furnish opportunity to follow the course of events connected with the constitutional and parliamentary history of France, 1789–1791, as seen from the point of view of the interior of the National Assembly.

A periodical, *La Gazette nationale: ou Le Moniteur universel*, was founded on 24 November 1789. It contained, in the form of résumés, information on foreign affairs and the debates in the National Assembly. On 3 February 1790 this journal absorbed the *Bulletin de l'Assemblée nationale;* and debates were reproduced in "dramatic form." At this same time, in anticipation of the binding of the first volume, *post factum* numbers were made up for the period from 5 May 1789, date of the convening of the States-General, to 24 November 1789. The journal was made official in the Year VIII, and its title was in 1811 shortened to the familiar *Moniteur universel.* It remained, with the exception of the period from 8 July 1814 to 1 February 1815, the official government journal until 1869. It was replaced at that time by the *Journal officiel,* which has continued to the present day. The *Moniteur universel,* having lost its official status, appeared as a conservative newspaper until 1901, at which time it went out of existence.

Covering largely the same ground as the first 275 numbers of the *Moniteur* are the first thirty-one volumes of the first series of the *Archives parlementaires* and the first eleven volumes of B.-J.-B. Buchez, and P.-C. Roux, *Histoire parlementaire de la Révolution française* (Paris, 1834). These volumes are the result of moderately scholarly synthesis. They are fuller but, from the nature of the case, less contemporary than the volumes of the *Moniteur.* Comparison of accounts in the three collections can be (and in the present study were) made where the effort may seem (or seemed) desirable.

Basic from a technical point of view to any collection is of course the official record, the *Procès-verbal de l'Assemblée nationale,* of which the first number begins with 17 June 1789. Like all similar sets of minutes, the *Procès-verbal* suffers from its skeletonlike character.

Other primary sources, such as memoirs, newspapers, and the like, are of tremendous volume. Sufficient reference to them may be found in any recent history dealing with the early Revolution. In the matter of newspapers, it may be recalled that Mirabeau on 2 May 1789 created a *Journal des Etats-généraux,* which was, upon the appearance of the seventh number, suppressed, but which was in effect continued as *Letters du comte de Mirabeau à ses commettants,* which in turn became, at the twentieth number, the *Courrier de Provence.* Certainly worthy of special mention is F.-A. Aulard, *La Société des Jaco-*

bins: Recueil de documents pour l'histoire du club de Jacobins de Paris (6 vols.; Paris, 1889–1897). For the text of the Constitution of 1791 as well as of subsequent constitutions, the best known collection is Léon Duguit and Henry Monnier (continued by Roger Bonnard), *Les Constitutions et les principales lois politiques de la France depuis 1789* (6th ed.; Paris, 1943).

There is, apparently, no monograph in French or English which treats the constitutional—or parliamentary—history of the period of the National Assembly of 1789–1791. The closest approach would seem to be Gaston Dodu, *Le Parlementarisme et les parlementaires sous la Révolution (1789–1799): Origines du régime représentatif en France* (Paris, 1911), which has something of the same particularity of subject for a considerably longer period. Worthy of special mention is the magistral essay by the late Léon Duguit, "La Separation des pouvoirs et l'Assemblée nationale de 1789," *Revue d'Économie politique*, VII (1893), 92–132, 336–372, 567–615. For different reasons, reference should be made to P. Duvergier de Hauranne, *Histoire du gouvernement parlementaire en France, 1814–1848* (10 vols.; Paris, 1857–1869). This work, of which the first three volumes appeared in a second edition in 1870–1872, deals in the first volume with the period before 1814. Although the account must be used with some caution, its conclusions are usually provocative.

In the early part of the present century, the Law Faculty of the University of Paris set as a subject of competition "Le Régime parlementaire en France sous Louis XVIII et Charles X.—Rechercher comment ont été introduits et appliqués, à cette époque, les principes et les usages de gouvernement de cabinet." Two well-known monographs that were crowned (Prix Rossi) were Louis Michon, *Le Gouvernement parlementaire sous la Restauration* (Paris, 1905), subsequently crowned by the Académie des Sciences morales et politiques (Prix Paul-Michel Perret), and Joseph Barthélemy, *L'Introduction du régime parlementaire en France sous Louis XVIII et Charles X* (Paris,

1904). Of these, the first is more historical, with the result that in the introduction some study, which is by no means without value, is made of the National Assembly of 1789–1791. Incidentally, the reading of this book suggested the present study.

References in the footnotes are in all cases to books of considerable, if inevitably uneven, value. No inference can be drawn from them as to which works proved most helpful. Inclusion is in nearly all instances prompted either by need to support a particular point or by the fact that a particular phrasing seems especially apt.

Aside from what is said above, a few random hints may be ventured for the political scientist who may be inclined to undertake some constitutional study in the period of the Revolution. If he begins with something in French, any one of several one-volume studies is to be recommended, of which some claim to being the best may be made for Georges Lefebvre, *La Révolution française* (new ed.; Paris, 1951). If he reads this and employs its excellent bibliographies, he will be well launched. If he prefers to begin in English, he will find a number of distinguished single-volume accounts that have appeared in the United States and Great Britain. No comparison unfavorable to American colleagues is involved in the hint that he may wish to select such a British author as J. M. Thompson, *The French Revolution* (New York, 1945), because the book is an excellent one and contains "a list of the fifty best books on the Revolution," or such as A. Goodwin, *The French Revolution* (London, 1953), because the little book is an excellent one and very recent. To conclude by returning to references to bibliographies, he will find, with respect to the background period, a convenient scholarly bibliographical note in Henry Bertram Hill, "French Constitutionalism: Old Regime and Revolutionary," *Journal of Modern History*, XXI (Sept., 1949), 222n, and, with respect to the earlier Revolutionary period, a useful note in George Gordon Andrews, *The Constitution in the Early French*

Revolution (*June to September, 1789*) (New York, 1927), pp. 5–8. Last but far from least, he will probably be moved to superlatives after consulting G. P. Gooch, "The Study of the French Revolution," pp. 259–296 in his *Maria Theresa and Other Studies* (London, 1951).

Index

ﺍﺳﺮﺍﺋﻴﻞ ١٩٨٢